Prejudice and Policymaking

Prejudice and Policymaking

Islamophobia in the United States and the Diffusion of Anti-Sharia Laws

Daniel Hummel

LEXINGTON BOOKS
Lanham • Boulder • New York • London

Published by Lexington Books
An imprint of The Rowman & Littlefield Publishing Group, Inc.
4501 Forbes Boulevard, Suite 200, Lanham, Maryland 20706
www.rowman.com

86-90 Paul Street, London EC2A 4NE

British Library Cataloging in Publication Information Available

Library of Congress Cataloging-in-Publication Data

Names: Hummel, Daniel, 1981- author.
Title: Prejudice and policymaking : Islamophobia in the United States and the diffusion of anti-sharia laws / Daniel Hummel.
Description: Lanham, Maryland : Lexington Books, 2021. | Includes bibliographical references and index.
Identifiers: LCCN 2021024425 (print) | LCCN 2021024426 (ebook) | ISBN 9781793612533 (cloth) | ISBN 9781793612540 (epub)
Subjects: LCSH: Muslims—Legal status, laws, etc.—United States. | Islamic law—United States. | Religious discrimination—Law and legislation—United States. | Islamophobia—United States. | Prejudices—United States. | Religion and politics—United States.
Classification: LCC KF4869.M86 H86 2021 (print) | LCC KF4869.M86 (ebook) | DDC 342.7308/5297—dc23
LC record available at https://lccn.loc.gov/2021024425
LC ebook record available at https://lccn.loc.gov/2021024426

Contents

Preface

It's an interesting exercise to reflect on how we got here. It has been nearly 20 years since the 9/11 terror attacks at the time of writing this. It would be an understatement to say that this was a critical inflection point. It's not that anti-Muslim fervor started that day. There were a number of terror attacks in the 1980s and 1990s committed by Muslims and then there was the Iranian Revolution in the late 1970s. Tension between the United States and the Muslim world is complicated and this is not the subject of this book. Instead, the focus is on Islam in the United States and those Muslims who call it home. They have become the focus of intense scrutiny over the decades and the target of those who see them as outsiders and potential threats. This has manifested in different ways with the focus of this book being on public policy and particularly the anti-Sharia laws.

If this is your first time hearing the word "Sharia" then this is a whole new world for you. In all likelihood you have heard of it in a negative way. It has been associated with "honor killings" and the brutality of the Taliban, a group that harbored Osama bin Laden, the leader of Al Qaeda and perpetrator of the 9/11 attacks. Following years of outright bigoted attacks on the Muslim community, Islamophobic movements have attempted to be "friendlier" to mainstream thought by arguing that this is not an attack on Islam or Muslims, but an effort to stop the spread of Sharia.

In the post-fact society, to quote Farhad Manjoo, it did not matter that there was no evidence of Sharia being implemented in the United States, at least in the way it is understood by opponents. All that mattered was there was a mosque on your street or a woman wearing hijab in the grocery store. When there were no factual stories to back up claims of a nefarious assault on American values, people on the internet just made them up and passed them off as fact. People searching for confirmation believed them immediately. It did not help that we had television networks that reported them as fact and people in political office who shared and promoted them.

It did not take long before this manifested in public policy. It just needed a policy window to pay credence to John Kingdon. That policy window became the so-called Ground Zero Mosque controversy in Manhattan in 2010. The reaction to the proposed project which was approved by the local community board was mostly imported from outside the community by those who saw it as a means to an end. The end was for the marginalization of the Muslim community and the bolstering of far-right politics in the United States. Linda Sarsour, the Palestinian-American activist and one of the founders of the Women's March in 2017, described it as the origin point of a renewed white nationalist fervor. This is how she described the atmosphere at the time, "As the controversy raged into the following year and then the next, it sometimes felt to me as if the very air had been poisoned, and my whole body ached from breathing in the hate."[1]

It is not a coincidence that in 2010 the first batch of anti-Sharia laws reached state legislatures. This book analyzes their passage by some states and tries to understand those factors that led to their introduction and why some states have them. Concordantly, one cannot understand these laws without understanding Islamophobia in the United States today. For those trying to understand this phenomenon in the United States particularly as it has manifested in the anti-Sharia movement this book is a valuable resource. Those studying public policy especially as it pertains to discriminatory legislation would find this an interesting read. For those fighting for the rights of Muslims in this country there is valuable information for understanding the threat. It should be understood that this threat is not only for Muslims, but for anyone that values their rights particularly religious freedom.

NOTE

1. Sarsour, Linda. 2020. *We Are Not Here to Be Bystanders: A Memoir of Love and Resistance* (New York: 37 Ink, 119).

Acknowledgments

Throughout the years there have been many that have influenced my research and how I think about the world. The multitude of activists that advocate for the civil rights and liberties of everyone in the United States have always impressed me with their tenacity and their ability to beat the odds. In my youthful inexperience I lacked the wisdom of the "long game" or the long arc of history and they have helped me put things in perspective. One day I may have your wisdom and patience.

Personally, Muslim organizations facing incredible odds in a country full with suspicion toward them amaze me with their resiliency and unflinching commitment to defend the Muslim community and other embattled communities. Anti-Muslim fervor has reached an all-time high with the goal of either subduing them or eliminating them all together. Unfortunately, it's a trend not isolated to the United States, but many countries around the world. For this reason, I dedicate this book to these unsung heroes who more often face demonization instead of praise.

In my academic life, I have met professors who have inspired me to write this book in good and bad ways. Those professors who acknowledged the institutional biases and problematic discourse toward Muslims in America while also exploring the diverse perspectives on this issue have been the most influential to me. Keep inspiring students to think critically about public policy and the impacts of prejudice.

I also want to thank the reviewers and editors of this book. Your guidance has helped to make this book worthy of publication. I would also like to thank my wife and son for being patient as I committed my time to this project. I hope the end result was worth it as I aimed to inspire critical thought on this important issue.

Introduction

Laila Abdelaziz was born and raised in Florida to immigrant parents from Palestine. Her youth was cut short with the events of 9/11. She knew that there had always been "Islamophobia," although that term was not being used as widely at the time, but it did not have the same characteristics as after 9/11. This event opened the door for a more amplified Islamophobia that necessitated the label.[1]

To Laila's dismay, not many in the Muslim American community pushed back on the bigotry being directed at them. This pushed her to advocate for better treatment and a more respectful dialogue. She became involved with Emerge USA, an organization founded by Muslims to increase engagement with the political process for their community. Today, this organization is known as EmgageUSA, which is one of the primary organizations mobilizing the Muslim vote.

While working for the organization as the Tampa Bay Regional Director, Laila became involved in lobbying against an anti-Sharia bill in Florida. This was her first time lobbying for anything and she was certainly not prepared for the political maneuverings of those who proposed and supported the bill. The bill did not seem to have any real substance, but that was not its purpose. Its purpose was to attack the Muslim community in Florida.

The bill was first introduced into Florida's legislature as HB 1273 in 2011. This first bill was subsequently postponed and withdrawn that same year. The following year, the House introduced HB 1209 which was approved in committee and on the House floor. This bill would go on to die in the Senate Judiciary Committee. This was the fate of HB 351 in 2013. By the time the fourth version of the bill appeared in the House Judiciary Civil Justice Sub-Committee in 2014 there was a significant push to get it signed into law. By that time, the bill had been limited to family law and passed this subcommittee and the respective House Judiciary Committee. The House approved the bill sending it to the Senate. The bill had a similar trajectory in the Senate leading it to the Senate Rules Committee where Laila lobbied against the bill.

Laila knew that the Democrats largely opposed the bill, although their opposition was not vigorous. The real fight, Laila thought, was to get some moderate Republicans to switch their vote. In retrospect, Laila observed many of the divisions in the Republican Party that came to characterize the Trump presidency in Florida at the time. There were some Republicans that were far-right supporting Christian nationalist narratives while others were more moderate with an emphasis on finance and economics. Many of these Republicans worried that some of the provisions of this law would negate international contracts that would hamper business.

Laila was hoping to kill the bill in committee. The votes in the committee were five Democrats to seven Republicans. All she needed was to have one Republican switch their vote and the bill would stall in committee. She was successful in this endeavor and it looked like the bill would, once again, fail in committee. At the last minute, a democratic lawmaker from Orlando, switched her vote and voted in favor of the legislation. Laila was flattened particularly since it had been a Democrat who turned the tide. The bill was then voted on by the Senate and sent to the Governor who then promptly signed it into law on May 14, 2014.

Laila would later learn that then Governor, Rick Scott, had called the senator and had offered money in the upcoming budget for an African American museum in Orlando in exchange for her vote. Not coincidently, she was also on the board of this museum. This was enough to switch a vote. Ironically, this money was never included in the next year's budget while the Governor got this bill signed into law.

This was not the end of the story though and is evidence of how efforts by people like Laila are turning the tide against this type of legislation. Before the final vote, amendment language was added to the bill which reduced the potential negative effect it could have on the Florida Muslim community. In particular it added this line, "The purpose of this section is to codify existing case law, and that intent should guide the interpretation of this section."

Foreign law, a more palpable term for Sharia, was not permitted in Florida courts for reasons of "strong public policy" and whether the law is unjust or unreasonable. Despite this language, the fact that the legislation confirms existing case law meant that more than a century of religious freedom law in Florida would prevent its targeting of Muslims. States tend to have a more expansive view of religious liberty than the Federal government.

This example from Florida shows the contentiousness of these bills and the fight over Sharia in the United States. The word "Sharia" comes from the Qur'an,[2] the holy book for Muslims. The word has been translated as the "clear path." It has been understood as the law of Islam not unlike the laws for other religious communities.

According to Hamid, Sharia is more secular than Christian conceptions of law in which it has conceptions of social justice, the rule of law and democratic politics. Hamid has also argued that nothing has bound the Muslim community like Sharia.[3] This means that Sharia is a critically important component to Islam and Muslim communities around the world. Any effort to ban Sharia is an effort to ban Islam and the very existence of the Muslim community.

Sharia is also not a rigid set of rules and regulations. Historically, it has been considered humanly shaped and in co-existence with state law and local norms.[4] It evolves over time despite being formalized by the four schools of thought in Islam (*madahib*).[5] The separation between the voluntary and the compulsory is not clear in the law.[6] There is detailed legislation, but is open to interpretation based on the goals and purposes of Sharia (*maqasid*).[7] In Islamic history and thought on Sharia there were two perspectives that informed the *maqasid*. The Ash'ari perspective used human reasoning to discover the divine law while the Mutazili perspective used legal rulings based on the spirit of the law to derive the ethical values from the divine law.[8] Both perspectives inform approaches to the Sharia today.

One prominent scholar in Islam that developed the *maqasid* was Al-Shatibi. He created a theory of *maqasid* that read the Qur'an inductively by asking, "What is the objective of this verse?" This approach was a challenge to the *usul-al-fiqh* approach to understanding the Qur'an and traditions in Islam. The formalization of Sharia by the schools of thought was an effort to create timeless rules known as *fiqh*.[9] *Fiqh* is the interpretation and application of the religious texts for the purposes of managing marriage, divorce, inheritance, business transactions and other matters.[10] Discussions on *fiqh* are more rigid than Sharia and are generally more unappealing to younger American Muslims. The rules in *fiqh* also happen to be the most cited for those aiming to ban Sharia without them realizing there is a difference between *fiqh* and Sharia.

Another component of *maqasid* is *maslaha* which can be translated as benefits, public interest or interest of humanity. *Maslaha* describe efforts to eliminate hardships, to satisfy needs and increase human wellbeing.[11] Any rule that would detract from the *maslaha* would need to be reevaluated from the perspective of the *maqasid*. The United States provides a fertile place for this reevaluation because of the religious freedom enshrined by the Constitution. The efforts to ban Sharia and thereby Islam is not only an affront to this religious freedom, but interrupts the process of evolution inherent in the Sharia.

An example of this evolution is the development of *Fiqh Al-Aqalliyyat*, which was developed by Shaykh Al-Alwami. This is jurisprudence for

Muslim minorities living in the West. This approach relies on the *maqasid* with interpretations based on the local context with references to the *maslaha*.[12] The development of this *fiqh* allows Muslim minorities living in the West to practice their religion while obeying the laws of the country. This is contrary to the narrative that Muslims are attempting to impose their laws upon the country. The free practice and interpretation of Islam in the United States allow these native interpretations.

Uddin noted that there are three categories of anti-Sharia laws. One group singles out Sharia as anti-American. The original version of these laws took this form. The second group mentions Sharia along with other religious legal traditions like halakhah. These are less common. The third group are laws that deny any consideration of foreign law in United States court rooms. This is the version finally adopted by the State of Florida and the most common versions of these laws.[13] Sharia, although not explicitly mentioned, is considered foreign law.

Mitchell and Toner studied the passage of these laws by the states and found conservativism as a predictor for them. The more conservative the people of a state were the more likely they were to pass these laws. In accordance, the size of the Evangelical Christian community also predicted their passage.[14] Their results confirmed a general problem of Islamophobia by traditional conservatives. American Muslims and their religion are considered a threat and the banning of Sharia is considered a preemptive step in stopping the processes of Islamization. Muslims are considered a deviant group by the morals and principles of traditional conservatives and therefore merit being restricted in their rights. In this way, their condition mimics the condition of other marginalized groups in the United States providing credence for an intersectional perspective.

Kimberlé Crenshaw created the term "intersectionality" in response to a court case that involved discrimination against African American women. In this case (*DeGraffenreid* v. *General Motors*) in 1976 the court determined that General Motors did not discriminate against black women because the company had hired both black men and white women. The court was unable to consider discrimination from a multi-dimensional perspective including both gender and race simultaneously. Intersectionality expanded conceptualizations of discrimination by arguing that some are treated unequally because they are at the cross-roads of different human experiences.[15] A woman could be discriminated against because of her gender, but a Muslim woman could be discriminated against even if gender-based discrimination is not evident.

In 2015 Crenshaw wrote an op-ed in the *Washington Post* about intersectionality. In it she recognized that oppression is experienced in different ways in the United States. A Muslim woman might experience discrimination in a unique way that other women do not experience it. This experience cannot be homogenized with other experiences. At the same time, intersectionality also stresses the inter-connectedness of discrimination. Crenshaw argued that movements for change need to work together. Those lobbying for racial justice should equally argue for gender justice according to this perspective.[16] Crenshaw wrote, "when they enter, we all enter."[17] The idea is that justice for one is justice for all. One cannot have equality for some, but not others.

Intersectionality has been criticized by those on the political Right and Left. Rothman, approaching the topic from the political Right, argued that it is Marxist in nature in which "class" has been substituted with "identity."[18] Instead of people engaging in class warfare, they engage in identity warfare with different marginalized identities against a dominant identity. Haidt, from the political Left, similarly argued that identity-based movements caused more harm than good. According to Haidt, these movements should be focused on "common-humanity identity politics" with shared morals and identities. In his book, Haidt referenced the effectiveness of Martin Luther King Jr. in using this approach to bolster the civil rights movement.[19]

Many American Muslims have approached the problem of Islamophobia from this perspective by trying to draw parallels between Islam and Christianity or to show how American Muslims are like everyone else. American Muslims with this outlook are attempting to tap into the American civil religion and thereby those shared morals and identities referenced by Haidt. The problem is that within the conservative movement in the United States today these ideas are rejected much like the controversy around the television show in 2011 on TLC "All-American Muslim."[20] Islam and thereby Sharia is the antithesis of the West.

This book is structured so that each of the probable factors for the introduction of anti-Sharia laws is considered based on the literature. Those states with these laws are compared to those states without them. This analysis helps to explain why some states have these laws and some states do not or why some states have introduced these laws at a higher frequency than other states. A version of this analysis was completed by the author of this book; however, in this book the data has been updated to 2019 with new levels of analysis and additional details have been added to provide more context.[21] In summary, the picture provided in this book is more comprehensive.

Chapter 1 provides some background on the anti-Sharia bills with some examples. As already discussed, there are at least three different versions of the bills. The problems with these bills are explained in this chapter when considering the Constitution and the history of religious freedom in the United States. A description of those states that have adopted these laws along with particular cases are also a part of this chapter.

Chapter 2 defines Islamophobia and how it is linked with orientalism and general racism. The source of prejudice toward Muslims today is explained as well as how it is the same and different to prejudice toward other groups. The role of 9/11 and the War on Terrorism is considered in this chapter as a major motivator of increased prejudice toward Muslims. In this environment the different political perspectives toward Islam and Muslims are explored and how some encourage a more Islamophobic perspective.

Chapter 3 is an exploration of the anti-Muslim groups in the United States that have promoted the anti-Sharia bills. This chapter introduces one of the major factors considered in the analysis for why some states have these laws. Lobbyists are considered important for whether a bill even gets introduced in the legislature. Some states have a greater presence of these groups than other states.

Chapter 4 explores the role of religious identity and presence as another factor. Evangelical Christians are more conservative and also more likely to support anti-Muslim legislation based on prior research. In addition, the size of the Muslim population is considered as a possible factor in whether a state has one of these laws. The theoretical reasons based on social contact and social dominance are explored in this chapter.

Chapter 5 follows the discussion in chapter 4 with a specific focus on religious salience as a separate factor. Religion is important in the lives of many people in the United States and religiosity determines its importance. There is some evidence that religious salience has been linked with prejudicial attitudes toward Muslims. This is explored in this chapter.

Chapter 6 is focused on the role of neighboring states in whether a state has an anti-Sharia law. A discussion on policy diffusion and its possible role in the spread of these laws is one of the focuses of this chapter. It is also one of the factors included in the analysis.

Chapter 7 is focused on the politics of these laws including the role of ideology, education and political competition. There is evidence that Islam is part of an ongoing "culture war" in the United States with Republicans and conservatives in general seeing Islam as a threat to the country and its values. Democrats are less likely to see it that way and are supportive of the Muslim community, in general. The professionalism of state legislatures is also considered in this chapter as a possible factor for having one of these laws.

Chapter 8 is the focus of the entire book with an analysis of the factors described from chapters 3 to 7. The design of the study including the variables in the analysis are described in this chapter. The results from this analysis are interpreted in this chapter with deference to chapter 9 for a more detailed explanation of the findings.

Chapter 9 is a summary of the analysis and the book, in general. It raises the "so what" question. There is an exploration of the lessons learned from the analysis including some predictions for the future. The lessons learned also extend to future studies on the topic in order to better understand the passage of these laws.

NOTES

1. Abdelaziz, Laila. Phone interview. October 27, 2020.
2. See Chapter 45, verse 18 in the Qur'an.
3. Hamid, Shadi. 2016. *Islamic Exceptionalism: How the Struggle Over Islam Is Reshaping the World.* New York: St. Martin's Press.
4. Ahmad, Irfan. 2010. "Genealogy of the Islamic State: Reflections on Maududi's Political thought and Islamism." *Islam, Politics, Anthropology*, 138–155.
5. Four schools of thought: Hanafi, Maliki, Shafii and Hanbali.
6. Ṣāfī, Lu'ayy. 2003. *Tensions and Transitions in the Muslim World.* Lanham: Rowman & Littlefield.
7. Popa, Eugenia L. 2012. "The Institution of State in Islamic Thought." *Scientific Annals of 'Alexandru Ioan Cuza' University of Iasi: Political Science*, 43–53.
8. Johnston, David. 2007. "Maqasid Al-Sharia: Epistemology and Hermeneutics of Muslim Theologies of Human Rights." *Die Welt des Islams 47*, no. 2, 149–187.
9. Rane, Halim. 2013. "The Relevance of a Maqasid Approach for Political Islam Post Arab Revolutions." *Journal of Law and Religion 28*, no. 2, 489–520.
10. Uddin, Asma T. 2019. *When Islam is Not a Religion.* New York: Simon & Schuster.
11. Johnston, *Maqasid Al-Sharia.*
12. Parray, Tauseef A. 2012. "The Legal Methodology of "Fiqh al-Aqalliyyat" and its Critics: An Analytical Study." *Journal of Muslim Minority Affairs 32*, no. 1, 88–107.
13. Uddin, *When Islam is Not a Religion.*
14. Mitchell, Joshua L., and Brendan Toner. 2016. "Exploring the Foundations of US State-Level Anti-Sharia Initiatives." *Politics and Religion 9*, no. 4, 720–743.
15. Crenshaw, Kimberlé. 1989. "Demarginalizing the Intersection of Race and Sex: A Black Feminist Critique of Antidiscrimination Doctrine, Feminist Theory and Antiracist Politics." *University of Chicago Legal Forum 1989*, no. 1, 139–167.
16. Crenshaw, Kimberlé. "Why intersectionality can't wait." *Washington Post* (Washington, D.C.), September 24, 2015. https://www.washingtonpost.com/news/in-theory/wp/2015/09/24/why-intersectionality-cant-wait/.
17. Crenshaw, *Demarginalizing the Intersection of Race and Sex*, 167.
18. Rothman, Noah. 2019. *Unjust: Social Justice and the Unmaking of America.* New York: Simon & Schuster.
19. Lukianoff, Greg, and Jonathan Haidt. 2018. *The Coddling of the American Mind: How Good Intentions and Bad Ideas Are Setting Up a Generation for Failure.* London: Penguin.
20. Mohammed, Shaheed N. 2015. "The Muslims Next Door: Transgressive Hybridity in TLC's All-American Muslim." *Mass Communication and Society 18*, no. 1, 97–118.
21. Hummel, Daniel. 2020. "Legislating Islamophobia: The factors for the existence of anti-sharia laws in the United States." *Public Policy and Administration*, 1–25. doi:10.1177/0952076720977610.

Chapter 1

Background on Anti-Sharia Bills

The United States began introducing and passing anti-Sharia laws in 2010. These laws are focused on prohibiting the application of Sharia in US courtrooms. Sharia is derived from the Qur'an, the Muslim holy book, and the Sunnah, the sayings and deeds of the Prophet Muhammad. It is widely applied across the Islamic world; however, its application is not uniform due to interpretations of it otherwise known as *fiqh*.[1]

David Yerushalmi, an Arizona attorney and founder of the Society of Americans for National Existence (SANE), drafted the model legislation in 2009 known as the American Law for American Courts (ALAC). Yerushalmi initially proposed a variant of the legislation in 2007 in which the observance of Sharia was considered an act of sedition, a felony punishable by up to 20 years in prison.[2,3] Frank Gaffney of the Center for Security Policy and the American Public Policy Alliance has supported the legislation. ACT! For America founded by Brigitte Gabriel has also supported the law. Yerushalmi, Gabriel and Gaffney are part of the "anti-Muslim inner circle" in a 2011 Southern Poverty Law Center (SPLC) report.[4]

Yerushalmi believes Muslims are holy warriors or at least sympathetic to holy war against non-Muslims.[5] He sees Sharia as the primary vehicle of this holy war and has dedicated himself to stopping its spread in the United States. He has argued that Sharia is a totalitarian ideology that undermines the Constitution.[6] He is unabashedly Islamophobic as well as racist and xenophobic.[7]

As expected, the laws have been challenged in court. The early version of the law was rendered unconstitutional due to Establishment Clause and Supremacy Clause issues. The language of these laws has changed in response with references to Sharia stricken; however, the intent of these laws is the same with some arguing that there remain Supremacy Clause issues.[8]

The version of the law spreading among the states has become known as the Kansas–Yerushlami model.[9]

Religious law has been used in the civil courts in the United States for some time by various religious communities. These "religious courts" enforce rulings through arbitration acts. Despite the religious nature of these courts and their decisions research has shown that their rulings closely align with secular courts.[10] As explained by Benhalim, "contrary to the concerns of the public discourse and past scholarship, religious courts that serve religious minorities tend to adapt to their secular surrounding, rather than the other way around."[11]

The attempt to ban Sharia is less about concerns over religious law and more about anti-Muslim prejudice. This was explained by Pedrioli, who observed that these, "laws discriminate against US Muslims out of whose religious tradition Sharia comes, and fail to offer an explanation for such discrimination, instead appealing to public ignorance of Islam and fear of terrorism."[12] Further, Prasatik added that, "laboring under the guise of protecting the US constitution and preventing future terrorist attacks, the singling-out of Islam has been described as plain bigotry."[13]

ADOPTING STATES

Between 2010 and 2019, 12 states adopted these laws. These include Alabama, Arizona, Arkansas, Florida, Kansas, Louisiana, Mississippi, North Carolina, Oklahoma, Tennessee, Texas, and South Dakota. See figure 1.1. One may notice that a majority of these states are in the South with a few in the Midwest and Southwest (only Arizona). The early adopters in 2010 were Louisiana,

Figure 1.1 States with Anti-Sharia Laws Enacted (2010–2019). Data from the Southern Poverty Law Center.

Oklahoma, and Tennessee. Oklahoma's law was a Constitutional Amendment referred to as the "Save Our State Amendment." This passed by referendum, but was overturned in Federal court in the case *Awad* v. *Ziriax*. The state then passed an anti-Sharia law in line with other adopting states in 2013. The last states to adopt these laws, so far, were in 2017 with Texas and Arkansas.

When looking at the number of times these bills have been introduced in state legislatures, 2011 was the high-water mark with the bill being introduced more than 50 times. Since then, the number of introductions has come down with peaks in 2013, 2015, and 2017. See figure 1.2. There have been only a handful of introductions in 2019 signaling that this wave of anti-Sharia law adoptions might be over.

Toward the end of 2016 some thought that states were finished with this law, but the election of Donald Trump gave new life to the movement.[14] This can be seen in 2017. It is unknown if this law is dead as there are many states that are similar to adopting states including neighboring states that have not adopted this law. Understanding why some states have this law while others do not is one of the purposes of the analysis in this book.

A cumulative hazard rate for law adoption indicates that the hazard has increased over time. The hazard rate is the conditional probability a state will pass an anti-Sharia law in a year. The number of states with anti-Sharia laws passed is divided by the number of states that have not passed these laws. As the number of states that have passed these laws have increased the ratio increases as well indicating the increase of probability of bill adoption in the other states. See figure 1.3.

Figure 1.2 Number of Anti-Sharia Bills Introduced Across All States (2010–2019). Data from the Southern Poverty Law Center.

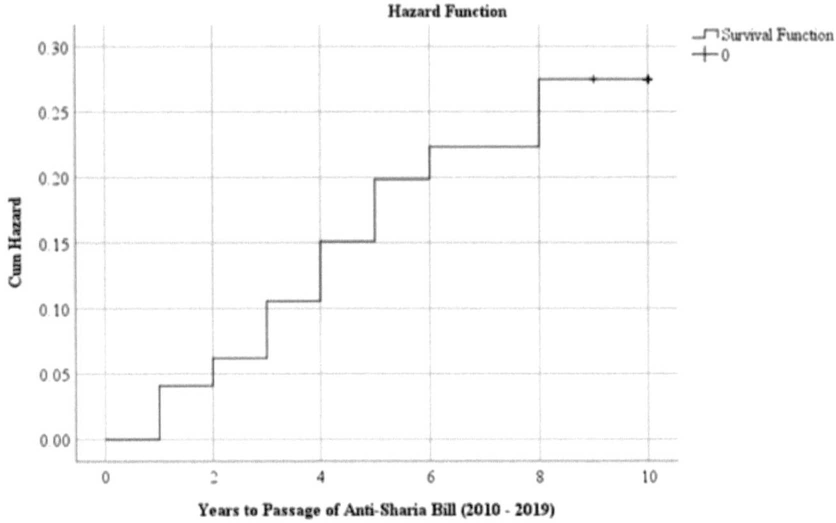

Figure 1.3 Cumulative Hazard Rate for Anti-Sharia Law Adoption (2010–2019). Data analyzed and projected by author.

In 2010 (year 0 in the figure), the cumulative hazard rate was 0 because the laws were just starting to be passed. By 2019 (year 10 in the figure), the rate was above .25; however, no anti-Sharia laws were adopted in this year. This means that by 2019 there was a greater than 25 percent probability of states adopting an anti-Sharia law. The steepest part of the figure is between years 2 and 6 (2012 and 2016, respectively) when the bulk of the states adopted the law. Since the hazard rate is simply based on whether other states have adopted the law, it does not consider other factors that may predict the introduction of these laws and eventual adoption. These factors are considered in the analysis in this book and are outlined in the separate chapters.

Andy's Law

Starting in 2013 another law with similar intentions to the anti-Sharia laws started to be passed by the same states that passed anti-Sharia laws. This law is known as Andy's Law. It was named after US Army Pvt. William Andrew "Andy" Long, who was killed outside an army recruiting center in Little Rock, Arkansas by Abdulhakim Muhammad in 2009. It was deemed a terrorist attack by a Muslim.

The laws have been promoted by ACT! For America. They allow people who were victims of terrorism to sue any entity deemed to be in material support. It gives the state authority to determine material support or essentially to determine organizations that it considers supportive of terrorism. The federal government already does this, but this legislation allows the state to go beyond this. With this legislation, a mosque or Islamic organization within the state can be accused as a supporter of terrorism which can then be sued by the family of terrorism victims for damages. Even if the lawsuit is spurious (of which it is most likely), the mosque or Islamic organization would spend thousands in legal fees defending itself in court. This is nothing short of a financial assault on Islamic organizations in the state in an effort to hobble them or get them to close their doors.

As of the writing of this book, only seven states have passed these laws. These include the same states that passed anti-Sharia laws with the exception of Kentucky. Alabama, Mississippi, Texas, South Dakota, Oklahoma, and Arizona which all have anti-Sharia laws have not passed this law. See figure 1.4.

The tactic of suing Muslim organizations for supposed links to terrorism by the victims of terrorism is something that has happened in Federal court. The most prominent case involved the parents of David Boim, who was killed in the West Bank in 1996. Using the Anti-Terrorism Act, the Boims won a verdict against several Muslim American organizations most prominently the Holy Land Foundation which was upheld in appellate court in 2008. Some of those organizations closed their doors because of bankruptcy due to the verdict. The Boims continued their legal suit in 2017 by suing the American Muslims for Palestine (AMP) which they argued was just an extension of the previous shuttered organizations. After a legal fight that lasted three years, the case was dismissed in US district court in 2020.

In Tennessee, former state senator Bill Ketron sponsored a bill in 2011 that operated like an Andy's Law, but was focused on Sharia. In this bill,

Figure 1.4 States with Andy's Laws Enacted (2010–2019). Data from the Southern Poverty Law Center

those who practiced Sharia were considered material supporters of terrorism.[15] The bill did not pass, but a version of Andy's Law did in 2015. This bill was also sponsored by Ketron. Tennessee has been a breeding ground for Islamophobic legislation in which it was one of the first states to pass an anti-Sharia law in 2010. This law as well as the one sponsored by Ketron is analyzed in the next section.

Anti-Sharia Bill Example: Tennessee

Senate Bill 1028 also known as the Material Support to Designated Entities Act attempted to create a list of Sharia practicing entities in the State of Tennessee. In the bill, Sharia is clearly linked with terrorism in which it states that terrorism is, "the result of a legal-political-military doctrine and system adhered to, or minimally advocated by, tens of millions, if not hundreds of millions of its followers around the world. This legal-political-military doctrine and system is known as Sharia."[16] Further, the legislation claims that Sharia, "requires all its adherents to actively and passively support the replacement of America's constitutional republic, including the representative government of this state with a political system based on Sharia."[17]

The bill establishes a link between Sharia and violence arguing that Sharia commands "jihad," an Arabic word commonly translated as "struggle" and can insinuate armed conflict. It is clear from the language of the bill that it is targeting Islam even if it claims that it does not prohibit the free exercise of Islam or target Muslims. Although the bill exhibits some understanding of what Sharia is, it does not understand the subtleties explored in this book or establish any factual link between those that adhere to Sharia principles and violence. The legislation is undoubtedly unconstitutional and infringes on the rights of Muslims in the State. This is explored later in the chapter.

The legislation establishes that the attorney general of the State is authorized to designate an entity as a Sharia organization. The bill than provides some avenues for the designated organization to apply for revocation of this designation. Those organizations that have been designated as a Sharia organization would have the same status as a terror organization and any material support would be considered a criminal offense. Punishment would be a fine, a 15-year jail sentence or both. If the "material support" resulted in the death of someone from a terror attack then the result would be life in prison.

This bill is an example of many of the early versions of the anti-Sharia laws that specifically targeted Sharia and thereby Islam. In the court case over Oklahoma's amendment (*Awad* v. *Ziriax*), this approach was considered unconstitutional. Following this ruling in 2012, the language of these laws changed in response. The word Sharia was replaced with "foreign law" and the focus became the inclusion of these laws in the state court system with a specific focus on family law.

A year prior to Ketron's law in Tennessee, Representative Vance Dennis proposed this version of the anti-Sharia law which was signed into law. In this way, Tennessee became a model for what type of anti-Sharia law would survive the legislative and legal process. This bill (HB 3768) established that any law or legal code from a foreign jurisdiction that violated the rights of citizens in the State of Tennessee based on its constitution and the constitution of the country would be null and void and therefore unenforceable. It was specifically written within the bill for the protection of minors as it pertained to custody arrangements.

Despite these limitations, the law also allows comity which is the recognition of foreign law, but only in circumstances where it and decisions made under it are not in violation of the Tennessee or United States Constitutions. In addition, the law also recognizes the right of people to form contracts under a foreign law even if it restricts their rights under the constitution. This last part is the most important as it establishes individual freedom, while the law still makes the case that preserving constitutional rights is the priority of the state. Finally, the law exempts corporations and other forms of business from compliance. This was one of the major concerns raised by moderate Republicans with the law which has been adopted in most versions of it across the states.[18]

Although these final provisions of the Tennessee law fall short of the exhortations in the Florida legislation discussed in chapter 1, it still provides some exemptions. The language in this bill is not as bigoted as that in SB 1028, but still problematic. First and foremost, even if it is not explicitly stated in the law the purpose of the law is to target Sharia in which it is seen as a "foreign law." Even if the law is purely symbolic, the statement that it sends to Muslims in Tennessee is quite clear, that is, their religion is not welcome.

Another troubling aspect of this law and others is that there is no evidence that "foreign law" has infiltrated a state's courts. There appears to be one case in New Jersey in 2010 where a Moroccan Muslim woman had entered into an arranged marriage and was subsequently abused by her husband. In court, the husband argued that his religion gave him permission to do those things and the judge denied a restraining order brought by his wife. This terrible decision was eventually reversed on appeal. Outside of this one case, there are no others.[19]

On the contrary, if implemented, these laws create new problems and actually hurt the rights and liberties they are purported to protect. On this point, Asma Uddin shared the story of Elham Soleimani who filed for divorce from her abusive husband in 2012 in Kansas. Elham had entered into a marriage contract with her husband based on the rules of Islam (Sharia) in which in the event of divorce, her husband owed her 1,354 gold coins or the equivalent of more than $600,000 dollars. Unfortunately for Elham, Kansas enacted its anti-Sharia law two months before and her contract could not be upheld in court because it represented "foreign law."[20]

Anti-Sharia Laws and Religious Freedom

Although there is a consensus on religious freedom as an important liberty in the United States, in practice it has been a contentious issue requiring numerous court cases to understand its limits. The first of these was *Reynolds* v. *US* (1879) which was the first court case on the free exercise of religion. In this case, Reynolds, who was a member of the Church of Jesus Christ of Latter-day Saints, married a second woman as permitted by the church at that time. He was charged with bigamy which he saw as an infringement on his freedom of religion. The court ruled against him citing that belief and action were separate and should be considered separately regarding legal claims to religious freedom. In this regard, the legislation that prevented plural marriages, the Anti-Bigamy Act, was constitutional because Congress had the authority to legislate on matters involving social duties and the need to maintain public order.[21]

This case became the standard for subsequent cases regarding free exercise until 1963 when Adell Sherbert, a Seventh-day Adventist, refused to work Saturdays per her religious duties and ultimately had difficulty securing employment. When she applied for unemployment benefits she was denied and considered ineligible. The case ascended to the Supreme Court (*Sherbert* v. *Verner*) who ruled in favor of Sherbert. This case established the "compelling government interest" criteria for determining if someone's free exercise of religion has been overburdened by an action of the state. This standard has served as one of the major sources for law on the free exercise of religion.

Greenawalt explained that, "if a law targets conduct because of its religious motivations or forbids conduct engaged in as a religious practice, while leaving unregulated similar conduct engaged in for nonreligious reasons, the state will never be able to show that the law is narrowly tailored to serve a compelling interest."[22] Dangerous religious activities could be forbidden by the government so long as those same secular activities are also forbidden. This standard also allowed a differential impact on different groups. This meant that if one religion had a dangerous religious practice while other religions did not this practice could be forbidden even if it only impacted that religious group. In addition, this standard also made it clear that there were no constitutional rights to religious exemptions.[23]

In 1990 the Supreme Court ruled on the firing of two Native Americans for the ingestion of peyote in practice of their religion (*Employment Division*

v. *Smith*). The court ruled against them by resurrecting the Reynolds case. In this, the court sided with the idea that religious practice whether marginal or central to that religion could be curtailed or forbidden entirely based on the idea that Congress had an obligation to maintain good order. In this, the restriction on the use of illegal substances is considered maintaining good order. Further, it was determined in this case that laws not passed to specifically target a religious group or its practices can be generally enforced against those groups.

The impacts of the Smith decision have been felt by religious communities. Following this decision, favorable decisions for free exercise claims reduced in the courts. According to the work of John Forren, religious claimants received protections only 1 out of 70 times.[24] The reduction in the efficacy of free exercise claims led many religious claimants to make free speech claims instead.[25]

Congress reacted swiftly to this decision by passing the Religious Freedom Restoration Act. The idea was that because the court gave wide latitude to more limits on religious practice by essentially overturning the Sherbert decision Congress had to reassert religious liberties as a primary and foundational freedom in the United States. It had bipartisan support.

The court responded to the legislation by declaring it unconstitutional. Congress had used the 14th Amendment which enshrines equal protections for all people in the country as a justification for their law. The court felt that this was a redefinition of rights which is not the jurisdiction of the legislative branch, but the judicial branch. Despite the law being stricken at the federal level, many states passed their own version of religious freedom restoration acts. These state-level acts left open methods of interpretation based on Sherbert or Smith.

Years later Congress responded to the crisis of the Smith decision for religious liberty by passing the Religious Land Use and Institutionalized Person's Act in 2000. This Act is focused on issues pertaining to the building of religious buildings and the practice of religion in prisons. The existence of this law has helped many religious communities deal with local efforts to thwart the building of places of worship. Uddin found that between 2010 and 2018 38 percent of claims made under this law were made by a Muslim community. This is considerable since the Muslim population in the United States is only around 1 percent of the total population. As Uddin explained the Muslim community has been forced to make compromises on their places of worship that have not been expected of other faith communities.[26]

The Smith decision supports majority-rule and conceives of equality from the perspective of sameness. Naturally this supports the dominant religion.[27] The fact that religious liberty claims are often made to reflect Christian priorities is an example of this.[28] True religious liberty is supportive of pluralism and diversity. One cannot talk one way about religious liberty when addressing one group and another way when addressing a separate group. It violates principles of equality. As argued by Mark Cladis, "The context for serious discussion of religion in the American public and political landscape is acknowledgment of the depth, breadth and diversity of America's religious landscape."[29]

Ultimately, this is a discussion about multi-culturalism. Multi-culturalism recognizes and institutionalizes differences in a society as a fact of life. From this perspective, cultural homogeneity is not only impossible to achieve, it is actually detrimental to society. Essentially, it represents the middle ground between individualism and communitarianism.[30]

Multi-culturalism is a divisive issue especially as other ways of life (cultures) are not equally respected which is sometimes derided as moral equivalence. However, the hypocrisy in a liberal society is difficult to overlook. This is something pointed out by Shadi Hamid in an article on the burkini. The burkini is a piece of clothing worn by Muslim women to go swimming without revealing their body. Basically, it's a wet suit, yet some people are so offended by it, for some reason, that they have called to ban it. For example, France has done this. Hamid argued that a liberal society must accept seemingly illiberal practices so long as they lead to no harm.[31] Many religious practices can be considered illiberal, but are protected religious freedoms.

Further, multi-culturalism as an idea has been considered a force for reducing inclusivity because the emphasis is on personal autonomy and constructing a liberal monoculture i.e. a shared liberal culture where dissent is very difficult.[32] This is why the backlash to multi-culturalism and liberalism in general among some faith groups has been so strong. Traditional conservatives view liberal egalitarianism with scorn because they naturally resist any idea that all ways of life should be respected equally.[33] Further, they see liberalism or secular humanism as another religion which is supported by the state.[34] Secularism, as the enforced separation of church and state, is seen from this prism even though legal secularism is different from secular humanism in the United States.[35] Muslims fall between these cracks in which they are a religious community demanding their rights to religious freedom while traditional conservatives devalue their way of life and therefore not worthy of protection. This has led to a contradictory approach to Islam.

Despite the legal standards and norms in the United States, the contradictory approach to Islam raises serious questions about the equal application of religious liberty standards. There has been a history in US courts of talking about Islam, the Qur'an and Muslims in anecdotal and insulting ways.[36] This bias has found expression in court decisions on free exercise. For example, Sisk and Heise found that in Federal courts between 1996 and 2005 non-Muslims won their cases 38 percent of the time while Muslims won their cases only 22 percent of the time.[37] The differential outcome with free exercise claims raises the accusation that religious freedom is not for everyone, but select groups which undermines the very principles of the Constitution and legal thought on it.

This also shows how the characterization of Islam and Muslims in society has real consequences for the rights and liberties of Muslims. As explained by Sisk and Heise, "the results of this study suggest that federal judges are not immune to the fears and suspicions often directed toward Muslims in American public life."[38] The Constitution does not differentiate between religions for its protections of religious liberty. Quite the contrary, religious liberty is applicable to Islam as Muslims were specifically mentioned by Thomas Jefferson, who used the Virginia Statute for Religious Freedom to frame the free exercise part of the First Amendment.[39] However, in practice, the different standards for upholding religious liberty have limited its scope. Despite these limitations the United States remains one of the freest countries for the practice of religion. This freedom has attracted immigrants from around the world including Muslims. For this reason, Muslims have expected equal treatment before the law to practice their religion.

The courts have ruled that there can still be differential impacts upon religious communities. These disproportionate impacts still have to abide by a strict scrutiny standard under compelling government interest. In this regard, while maintaining good order only religious practices that are dangerous and thereby violate this good order can be limited by the government. This is why many opponents of Islam and Muslims frame Islam as a dangerous religion in which regular practice of it leads one to become extreme and violent. Based on this understanding, these opponents recommend severe limits on Muslim free exercise through such things as the anti-Sharia laws.

Quite frankly, Muslim free exercise is often dismissed even when it aligns with similar claims by Christian groups. For example, Somali cab drivers in Minneapolis decided that they were not going to take passengers carrying alcohol from the airport. Alcohol is forbidden in Islam. The response in the media and by government was swift and condemnatory with penalties for not taking passengers. The case went to court and the cab drivers lost.[40] In other cases involving Christians denying services to someone for religious beliefs the courts have supported the religious claimant.

This contradictory approach to religious liberty brings us back to Tennessee in the heart of the "Bible Belt." In Murfreesboro, Tennessee a local group of Muslims aimed to build a mosque along with other facilities and had applied for permits from Rutherford County. The community split on the issue after the planning commission approved the project with some outside Islamophobic groups using the issue as a lightning rod to fuel anti-Muslim hate.

The controversy led to a local court case (*Estes* v. *Rutherford County Regional Planning Commission*) in 2010 around the same time as the Ground Zero Mosque controversy. The judge in this case entertained arguments that Islam is not truly a religion and therefore not deserving of the same First Amendment protections as other religious groups. It was argued that Islam is a geopolitical system and an antithesis to American values as well as a general threat to the community. This same diatribe is echoed within Ketron's 2011 Material Support law.[41] Bill Ketron is currently mayor of Rutherford County.

The propensity to deny Muslims access to the same rights and liberties as others in the United States should alarm people who value these rights and liberties. As Uddin explained, "if we start weakening the legal protections for religious freedom because we think religious freedom is protecting all the wrong beliefs, we'll soon enough find ourselves in a place where the law fails to protect much at all."[42] Anti-Sharia laws should be seen from this perspective.

NOTES

1. Pedrioli, Carlo A. 2012. "Constructing the other: U.S. Muslims, anti-Sharia law, and the constitutional consequences of volatile intercultural rhetoric." *Southern California Interdisciplinary Law Journal 22*, no. 1, 65–108.

2. Ali, Wajahat, Eli Clifton, Matthew Duss, Lee Fang, Scott Keyes, and Faiz Shakir. 2011. *Fear, Inc.* Washington, DC: Center for American Progress. https://www.americanprogress.org/issues/religion/reports/2011/08/26/10165/fear-inc/.

3. Elsheikh, Elsadig, Basima Sisemore, and Natalia R. Lee. 2018. *Legalizing Othering: The United States of Islamophobia*. Berkeley, CA: Haas Institute. https://haasinstitute.berkeley.edu/sites/default/files/haas_institute_legalizing_othering_the_united_states_of_islamophobia.pdf.

4. Steinback, Robert. 2011. *Jihad Against Islam*. Montgomery, Alabama: Southern Poverty Law Center, 2011, https://www.splcenter.org/fighting-hate/intelligence-report/2011/jihad-against-islam.

5. "David Yerushalmi: A Driving Force Behind Anti-Sharia Efforts in the U.S." *Anti-Defamation League*. Last modified 2012. https://www.adl.org/resources/profiles/david-yerushalmi.

6. Patel, Faiza, Matthew Duss, and Amos Toh. 2013. *Foreign Law Bans: Legal Uncertainties and Practical Problems*. Washington, DC: Center for American Progress. https://www.brennancenter.org/sites/default/files/publications/ForeignLawBans.pdf.

7. Anti-Defamation League, "David Yerushalmi."

8. Sheeder, Renee. 2013. "Awad v. Ziriax: The tenth circuit's defense against the power of religious majority factions." *Denver University Law Review 90*, no. 3, 801–823.

9. Patel, Duss & Toh, *Foreign Law Bans*.

10. Benhalim, Rabea. 2019. “Religious Courts in Secular Jurisdictions: How Jewish and Islamic Courts Adapt to Societal and Legal Norms.” *Colorado Law Scholarly Commons* 84, 745–800.

11. Ibid., 747.

12. Pedrioli, *Constructing the Other*, 69.

13. Prasatik, Sara. 2013. “Assessing the viability of state international law prohibitions.” *Houston Journal of International Law 35*, no. 2, 466.

14. Beydoun, Khaled A. 2017. “‘Muslim Bans’ and the (re)making of political Islamophobia.” *University of Illinois Law Review*, no. 5, 1734–1774.

15. The Tennessean (Nashville). “Dozen of legislators pushed copycat anti-Sharia bills. Murfreesboro’s Bill Ketron was one of them.” July 19, 2019. https://www.tennessean.com/story/news/2019/07/19/tennessee-bill-ketron-copycat-anti-sharia-law/1767805001/.

16. Ketron, Bill. *Material Support to Designated Entities Act*. Nashville: Tennessee Senate, 2011. https://www.capitol.tn.gov/Bills/107/Bill/SB1028.pdf, 2.

17. Ibid, 2.

18. Dennis, Vance. *As enacted, establishes certain public policies in regard to the application of foreign laws, legal codes and systems to protect constitutional rights of citizens of this state*. Nashville: Tennessee General Assembly, 2010. https://wapp.capitol.tn.gov/apps/BillInfo/Default.aspx?BillNumber=hb3768&ga=106.

19. Shanmugasundaram, Swathi. *Southern Poverty Law Center* (blog). February 5, 2018. https://www.splcenter.org/hatewatch/2018/02/05/anti-sharia-law-bills-united-states.

20. Uddin, Asma T. 2019. *When Islam Is Not a Religion*. New York: Simon & Schuster.

21. Greenawalt, Kent. 2009. *Religion and the Constitution, Volume 1: Free Exercise and Fairness*. Princeton: Princeton University Press.

22. Ibid, 38.

23. Ibid.

24. Forren, John P. “In Smith’s Wake: The Impact of the United States Supreme Court’s Peyote Decision in the Lower Courts.” PhD diss., The Johns Hopkins University, 2001.

25. Claborn, David. 2011. “Effects of Judicial and Legislative Attempts to Increase Religious Freedom in U.S. State Courts.” *Journal of Church and State* 53, no. 4, 615–634.

26. Uddin, *When Islam Is Not a Religion*.

27. Haun, William J. 2020. “Religious Liberty and the Common Good.” *National Affairs*, no. 44, 132–151.

28. Koppelman, Andrew. 2018. “How Could Religious Liberty be a Human Right?” *International Journal of Constitutional Law* 16, no. 3, 985–1005.

29. Cladis, Mark S. 2008. “Painting Landscapes of Religion in America: Four Models of Religion in Democracy.” *Journal of the American Academy of Religion* 76, no. 4, 879.

30. Durante, Chris. 2012. “Religious Liberty in a Multicultural Society.” *Journal of Church and State* 54, no. 3, 323–352.

31. Hamid, Shadi. "The Dilemma of the Burqini." *The Atlantic*, July 20, 2017. https://www.theatlantic.com/international/archive/2017/07/burqini-reactions/533715/.

32. Durante, *Religious Liberty in a Multicultural Society.*

33. Koppelman, *How could religious liberty be a human right?*

34. Merriman, Scott A. 2015. "What should the scales of justice balance? Historical aspects of the religious liberty debate." *Faulkner Law Review* 7, 79–103.

35. Joppke, Christian. 2016. "Beyond the wall of separation: Religion and the American state in comparative perspective." *International Journal of Constitutional Law* 14, no. 4, 984–1008.

36. Failinger, Marie A. 2012. "Islam in the Mind of American Courts: 1800 to 1960." *Boston College Journal of Law & Social Justice* 32, no. 1, 1–29.

37. Heise, Michael, and Gregory C. Sisk. 2013. "Free Exercise of Religion Before the Bench: Empirical Evidence from the Federal Courts." *Notre Dame Law Review* 88, no. 3, 1371–1408.

38. Ibid, 237.

39. Freeman, Marsha B. 2017. "Holier Than You and Me: 'Religious liberty' is the new bully pulpit and its new meaning is endangering our way of life." *Arkansas Law Review* 69, 881–909.

40. Ahmed, Sameer. 2014. "The religious right to refuse service: Accommodating Muslims in a 'Christian' America." *Albany Government Law Review* 7, 379–314.

41. Uddin, *When Islam is Not a Religion.*

42. Ibid, 310.

Chapter 2

Islamophobia

Dr. Saleh Sbenaty, who is a faculty member at Middle Tennessee State University, joined the Murfreesboro community in 1993. At the time there were around 12 Muslim families in the area, but it was growing. Rutherford County, a suburb of Nashville, was one of the fastest growing counties in the United States in the early 1990s. Despite this recent growth, there had been a nascent Muslim community there since the 1980s.

The growth in the Muslim community meant that there was a need for a larger place to pray. Up until that moment, the community had prayed in an apartment, a converted garage and a small building purchased in 2003. Eventually, the community was able to pool their resources enough to purchase some land next to a church in 2009 for the future site of the Islamic Center of Murfreesboro. It was an occasion for celebration as the community would finally have a place designed specifically for them. The community put up a sign marking the occasion indicating that the empty piece of land was the future site of the mosque. Saleh reflected on the moment:

> Having been in the community for so long, we had nothing but good experiences. Going back to 9/11, the majority of the community across the county experienced backlash, but we had a coalition of interfaith groups that started a really beautiful conversation among people of faith. We felt like we were part of the community and we never had an issue with Islamophobia, until we put the sign up.[1]

When the leadership of the Muslim community developed the site plan and submitted it for approval from the county commissioners, it was approved by all of them. There was no controversy with the site at the time. The zoning allowed it and the application was full proof. The local newspaper reporter was at the planning meeting and reported on all of the decisions as is usual. However, when news of the mosque's approval hit the newspapers the next day, it was anything but usual for some in the community.

During one of the meetings of the mayor and commissioners at the county courthouse, some people stormed the meeting. They were clearly upset over their approval of the mosque. They began making claims that Islam was not a religion and therefore it did not deserve the same constitutionally protected rights as "real" religions. Some claimed that the mosque would be a breeding ground for extremism and that the Muslims in the community were there to kill them.

Saleh and others in the Muslim community were clearly shaken by this mob, but they felt that it was just the knee-jerk reaction of some misinformed people in the community. In good faith, the mosque hosted an open house in which 400 people came in support. Not everyone was there in support though as some came to tell the Muslims and those that were there to support them that they worship the Devil. The leadership of the mosque opted to respond amicably to these people and left them to their task in the hope that they would see their error and reconcile with the Muslim community. As Saleh said in retrospect, "We were naive at the time. We thought we could level with these people."[2]

Not long after the open house, there was a rally against the mosque. The leadership of the mosque kept thinking that this was a short-term outburst and chose not to engage in a counter-demonstration. It is easy to imagine that this type of thinking was what frustrated Laila so much in Florida following the 9/11 attacks and the complacency in the Muslim community.

Unfortunately, it did not go away. Instead, it escalated with vandalism at the mosque and lawsuits claiming that the process for approval of the mosque was flawed. The infamous court case, *Estes* v. *Rutherford County Regional Planning Commission*, introduced into court the first time the claim that Islam was not a religion, the same claims that protestors made when they stormed the county courthouse. To back up their claims in court, various "experts" on Islam were presented who are popularly known as the "Who's Who of Islamophobes" by the Southern Poverty Law Center.[3] This included Robert Spencer, Frank Gaffney, and Pamela Gellar.

Eventually the judge voided the site permit on procedural grounds and while the mosque had been completed, the Muslim community could not occupy it. This warranted the intervention of the Department of Justice at the Federal level using the power invested in it by the Religious Land Use and Institutionalized Persons Act. A lawsuit was filed against the county and a restraining order was issued permitting a temporary permit of occupancy. The Muslims of Murfreesboro, Tennessee were finally able to pray in their mosque after a three-year fight.

Saleh reflected on this dark period in Murfreesboro and observed that things have gotten better since that time despite having one of the architects of the state's anti-Sharia law as the current mayor of the county. Saleh, like Laila, believes that what he observed during those years was a precursor to the wave of white nationalism that hit Washington, DC with the election of Donald Trump. The same that was observed by Linda Sarsour in New York City with the so-called Ground Zero Mosque. Saleh made this startling confession:

> I swear to God, I am so depressed. I left my country (Syria) for the sake of freedom. I came here almost 40 years ago and seeing the country transforming itself into anarchy and dictatorship, it really depresses me.[4]

ISLAM IN THE UNITED STATES

It's hard to understand the visceral reaction to the proposed mosque in Murfreesboro considering that Muslims had been there for several decades. In general, the United States is home to one of the most diverse Muslim populations in the world. Many Muslims from all over the world came to the United States voluntarily and involuntarily like Saleh and his family. The earliest Muslims were the slaves who came from North and West Africa in the tens of thousands. Many of these slaves who had been captured in wars between Muslims on the African continent were educated and literate. During the slave trade, many were relocated to Georgia and South Carolina which had the greatest concentrations of Muslim slaves. As time passed, their children lost their connection with Islam and the religion ceased to be practiced among their descendants during and following slavery.[5]

During the first two decades of the twentieth century, some of the earliest Muslim immigrants began to make their way to the United States from Anatolia, the Levant, Eastern Europe, and Asia. Many of these populations came from the former territories of the Ottoman Empire which was collapsing creating chaos, unrest, and violence especially targeting Muslim minorities. The United States offered a refuge from this as well as a place of great opportunity. For example, many came from Albania especially following the Balkan Wars in 1912. Muslims were not the only people to flee these areas. The majority of immigrants to the United States from the former Ottoman territories were Christian. Due to the draconian immigration laws in the United States at the time and the deep-seated suspicion and hatred toward Muslims, many Muslims attempted to hide their identity and fit in with their Christian compatriots.[6]

It became apparent to these early Muslim communities that if they were to perpetuate their Islamic identity they would need to develop Islamic institutions. Between World War I and II Muslims began to develop these institutions. Most of the time this took the form of building mosques. Large scale Islamic associations did not begin to develop until the 1950s and 1960s.[7] The first of these associations was the Federation of Islamic Associations which can be seen as a predecessor to the present-day Islamic Society of North America. It was also during this time that the United States liberalized its immigration laws with the Hart-Cellar Act of 1965. Following its passage and implementation, many educated Muslims began to immigrate to the United States to seek better opportunities.[8]

Around this time, a large number of African Americans began to convert to Islam. For many this was reconnecting with their original religion before they were enslaved and brought to the United States. They originally embraced local variants of Islam like Moorish Science and the Nation of Islam. Malcolm Little also known as Malcolm X was the most famous convert to the Nation of Islam following World War II. Later, in the 1960s following Malcolm's exit from the Nation into mainstream Sunni Islam and the death of its original founder Elijah Muhammad, his son, W.D. Mohammed moved the following into mainstream Sunni Islam. Most African American Muslims today are adherents of this version of Islam.[9]

Today, Muslims are in every state with some states having more than others. According to the Association of Religion Data archives, Texas, New York, Illinois, California, and Virginia have the most Muslims by the number of adherents as of 2010.[10] Vermont, Montana, Hawaii, North Dakota, and Wyoming have the least amount of Muslims. See figure 2.1 for the states in order of the number of Muslims. The average is demarcated on the graph.

Muslims in the United States have been working to develop their identity as both Muslims and Americans. Peek observed that initially Muslims only saw Islam as an ascribed identity in which they were born into it. The earliest Muslims in the United States likely had this perspective. Later, Islam became a chosen identity as Muslims reconnected with their religion. Finally, Muslims began to declare their identity through physical markers and verbal declarations. This happened especially after the 9/11 terror attacks as Islam and Muslims became the subject of attack.[11] Some Muslims like Laila began to feel the pressure of the moment and the very survival of the Muslim community was on the table.

This is not to say that the process was linear and that American Muslims are now proud and open about being Muslim. O'Brien referred to Muslim identities in the United States as "stigmatized" with significant social costs from identifying as a Muslim. Muslims will often try to manage this stigma in what O'Brien labeled "stigma management rehearsal." This is the

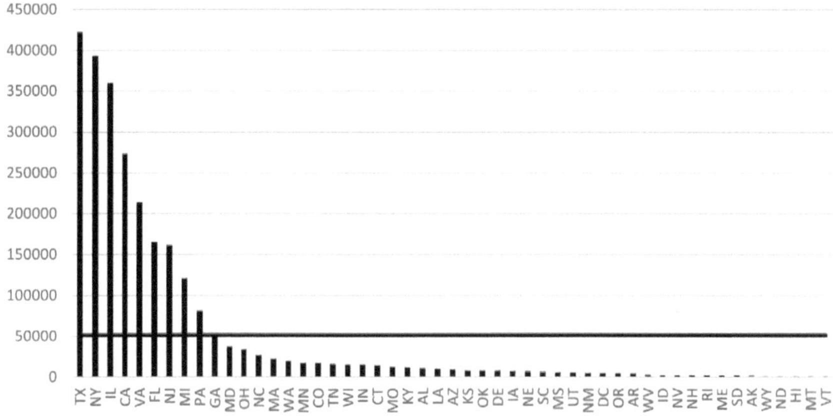

Figure 2.1 States by the Number of Muslims in 2010. Data compiled from Association of Religion Data archives.

anticipation of stigma related to their identity as Muslims and how they will respond to it. Most of the time this is nonverbal or nonphysical. People will give a kind of look that has been described as a micro-aggression. Adults are not as affected by it as the youth which has raised many concerns about the well-being of Muslim youth in the United States.[12]

In this environment Muslims have developed a hybrid identity in which they are both Muslim and American. They are more Muslim in some contexts and more American in others. The idea of even being an American Muslim is considered by some to be transgressive and outside the boundaries of Americanness. The fact that sometimes Muslims who were born and raised in the United States have to establish themselves as American and not "foreign" has been challenging for this community.[13]

It has also mobilized it to change this situation. The political involvement and integration of the American Muslim community has unsettled those with anti-Muslim beliefs. In the 1990s at the beginning of American Muslim mobilization Samuel Huntington and Bernard Lewis argued that Islamic civilization was a threat to the West. This argument gained popularity as the threat from Communism subsided and the Cold War ended. The Council on American Islamic Relations was established at this time to confront this sentiment and advocate for Muslim rights. Today, there seems to be no shortage of those who are arguing that Islam is the antithesis of the West and that Muslims in the West are part of a "silent jihad" to overturn secular Western governments and replace them with an Islamic state. This attitude or disposition has been described as Islamophobia.

DEFINING ISLAMOPHOBIA

According to Cesari, the term "Islamophobia" was first used in 1922 by Nasreddine Dinet, a French painter and convert to Islam.[14] Others have attributed the term to French colonial authorities in 1910 who used the term "Islamophobie" to describe an unhelpful attitude toward Muslims in French African colonies.[15] Much later, the term was used again in 1997 in the Runnymede Report in the United Kingdom.

The term is controversial, yet there has been no better term to describe anti-Muslim sentiments. The term alludes to an irrational fear of Muslims, yet those that exhibit anti-Muslim attitudes assert there is nothing irrational to their fear of Muslims. These same individuals also claim the term is used to silence critics of Islam. Despite these criticisms, "others point to the analytical usefulness and heuristic accuracy of the concept, prone to capturing and disclosing hostile and discriminatory attitudes and practices toward Muslims."[16] The term is used to capture the fear, negativity and hostility directed at Muslims by those that claim Islam is an antithesis to American values.[17]

Further, Islamophobia is believed to be the next evolution of Orientalism or anti-Arab racism with such ideas as the "clash of civilizations."[18] Its linkages with Orientalism not withstanding and maybe because of this transition, Islamophobia is different from Orientalism. Orientalism was not entirely negative in which there was a fascination with the East in the West. Orientalism also encompassed Western attitudes toward Jews. This is not the case today. Narratives around racial dominance by European colonial powers especially toward the Muslim other began to develop in the nineteenth century, which may have led some French authorities to begin calling it "Islamophobie" in the early twentieth century. According to Kalmar, this crystallized in the twenty-first century.[19]

The dichotomy between "good" Muslims and "bad" Muslims has developed out of this movement.[20] The problems in the Muslim world have been reduced to the idea that the rise of terrorism is directly linked to a faithful implementation of Islam. This means that conservative Muslims are considered mostly "bad" Muslims who support terrorism. This is because Islam is considered a violent authoritarian religion which has a political agenda intent on destabilizing the West. Islamophobia, or the fear of Islam, is built around these ideas that Islam is a threat to non-Muslims.

An example of this attitude can be highlighted through the words of Nassim Taleb. Taleb, a Greek Orthodox Christian from Lebanon, described Salafi Muslims as dangerous and an intolerant minority in the West.[21] Salafi Muslims are conservative Sunni Muslims, who may be likened to orthodox believers in other religions. Some Salafis have engaged in violence (not unlike believers in other religions), but most can be referred to as "quietist Salafis," who are more concerned about the rituals of prayer and hygiene than politics.[22] Most alarmingly, Taleb refers to them as outright enemies of Christians and Jews and argues that the West is "committing suicide" by allowing this group religious freedom. Basically, any observant Sunni Muslim is a Salafi who is an enemy of the West and does not deserve the same religious freedoms as other groups. This argument is at the core of the anti-Sharia laws.

THE SOURCES OF ISLAMOPHOBIA

Allen wrote an extended analysis on the meaning of Islamophobia. In this work, he explained that Islamophobia has three sources. The first source is the general stereotypes about Muslims and Arabs that have proliferated through time. These stereotypes are also part of out-group subordination explained through concepts like social dominance and supported by various ideologies.[23] The "clash of civilizations" thesis fits into this framework because of its emphasis on conflict and the need of one culture or civilization to dominate another. Those who possess these beliefs cannot imagine the existence of Muslim communities in the West unless they are thoroughly dominated by the mainstream culture and / or their culture and religion is assimilated out of existence.

The second source Allen explained is the existence of representation. History and culture have communicated meaning through the generations. Allen specifically mentioned semiology which emphasizes the importance of signs in providing meaning that is transmitted through the generations.[24] A perspective developed in Medieval Europe regarding Islam and Muslims that was also shaped by the spread of Christianity. At this time the Islamic world was thriving and Muslim armies had invaded Spain. There were also reports that the Fatimid caliph, Al-Hakim bi-Amr Allah, who was also ruler of Palestine, oppressed Christians and destroyed many churches including the Church of the Holy Sepulchre, the holiest site in Christianity. This led to the justification for the launch of the Crusades. These events reverberate with Christians and Muslims until this day.

The third source discussed by Allen is related to general racism. In the United States race has been an important distinction between people. This has been based on skin color, but can be extended to cultural markers that are linked to religious belief. Through differentiation, exclusionary policies can be implemented to enforce this differentiation and disadvantage one group over another.[25] Given that most Muslims are "people of color" and that some black liberation movements embraced Islam as a means to this liberation,

Islam has been associated with racial and ethnic minorities in the West. This association has made the conversion of white people to Islam a transgressive act where their "whiteness" is even questioned in society.[26]

Those with Islamophobic beliefs reject any notion that they are racist because they argue Islam is not a race. Racism is a mentality that may or may not have any linkage with race. Love argued that Islamophobia is a racialized phenomenon. Muslims have a particular appearance based on clothing, skin color and accents that allow them to be "raced."[27] This allows Muslims to be treated differently because of this.

Further Garner and Selod defined racism by three elements, ideology, power relationships and discrimination. These elements are closely related to many of the elements of Islamophobia detailed by Allen. They argued that Muslims can be "raced" because Islam emphasizes practices that change their outward appearances through wearing certain types of clothing. Muslims also are represented by people from certain geographical locations which display physical and cultural characteristics as explained by Love.[28]

Racialization also means that Muslims can be homogenized by the dominant group. This allows stereotypes and other forms of degradation to be expressed toward them as a group. These have been captured by certain expressions like, "Muslims are terrorists." Islam began to be associated with terrorism around the same time the Muslim community began to grow and integrate in the United States. This narrative allowed people to disparage Muslims and Arabs on the grounds that they were perceived threats and therefore gave credence to their acts of differentiation and oppression. As explained by Garner and Selod, "using racialization as a key analytical concept allows us to make sense of the fact that regardless of physical appearance, country of origin and economic situation, Muslims are homogenized and degraded by Islamophobic discourse and practices in their everyday lives."[29]

Religion offers another form of identity that is difficult to extract from race. The association of Islam with "people of color" is an example. In their study, Hewstone et al. found that social dominance played a role in predicting greater levels of Islamophobia.[30] Social dominance applies to racial dominance, but extends to religious dominance with the close association of religion with race. The racialization of Muslims allows them to be defined as an out-group. Ideology and stereotypes reinforce this as Muslims are seen as a threat to the in-group.

The theological differences matter for the most religious who are also in the business of winning hearts and minds to their religion. Islam and Christianity offer competing theologies which are both missionary faiths. Hewstone et al. found that as religious salience increased there were greater levels of Islamophobic sentiment. This meant that as religiosity increased so did Islamophobic views. They may justify the oppression of the out-group to silence discordant messages. Islam directly challenges core Christian theological concepts like the death of Jesus and the Trinity.

Islamophobia fits the racial and cultural separation in the United States along with foreign and domestic policy that allows the authorities to take a hard line against Muslim communities. As explained by Love, "'Islamophobia' is the latest term for a centuries-long history of American state policy, cultural discourses, and discriminatory practices that enforce racial boundaries around Middle Easterners in America."[31] The terrorist attacks on 9/11 did not change this discourse, but confirmed it.

Interestingly, Christopher Bail found that attitudes toward Islam were actually more favorable following 9/11 compared with today.[32] This change in attitudes is the result of the assertion of Islamophobic narratives over time since the attacks. It has got to the point that as observed by Saeed Khan, "The level of acrimony toward Muslims and Islam has attained a new intensity, and even the ambivalent have decided to take a side in the debate, often toward antipathy."[33]

It does not help that Muslims have a lack of social and political capital.[34] Any social and political capital they had prior to 9/11 has deteriorated since then.[35] This was the finding of Bail. Anti-Muslim groups have considerable influence over the media, government and public opinion while mainstream Muslim organizations have lost influence.[36] This has made Muslim Americans easy targets for public scorn and discrimination.

DISCRIMINATION AND SHARED EXPERIENCES

The discrimination experienced by Muslims in the United States is not unique in which there are shared experiences with other groups. For example, Kalkan et al. found that views of other cultural groups predict attitudes toward Muslims including views of other minority faiths.[37] One of these religious groups is the Church of Jesus Christ of Latter-day Saints (LDS) otherwise known as the Mormons. There is a shared experience of religious discrimination between Muslims and Mormons. Mormons themselves have been open to immigrants in which Utah, the only state with a majority of Mormons, has a relatively liberal immigration policy for a predominantly Republican state.[38] Similarly, Uddin noted that Republican politicians and lawmakers in every state have made anti-Muslim statements except in Utah.[39] Consequently, Penning found that there is a significant overlap in negative views about Mormons and Muslims.[40]

Penning argued that there are three reasons for the negative views about these two religious communities. The first reason is the portrayal of these communities by the media. He especially noted that this has led to more negative views about Muslims. Cesari observed that the public discourse on Islam by the media and other sources has led to higher levels of Islamophobia.[41] The way the media has covered attacks by Muslims versus non-Muslims has been substantially different. Attacks by Muslims are more quickly labeled terrorism and due to their religious devotion.[42] The rhetoric in the media on Islam and Muslims has emboldened others to verbally and physically attack them especially following high-profile events that have involved Muslims like terror attacks.[43]

Hate crimes against Muslims have remained historically high according to the Federal Bureau of Intelligence's Uniform Crime Report.[44] In figure 2.2 three important events that have affected the American Muslim community and the years that followed are included in a graph of incidents of anti-Muslim hate crimes. These include the presidency of Donald Trump starting when he announced his candidacy in 2015 and ending in 2018, the last year of data, the 9/11 terror attacks in 2001 and the three years that followed them, and the Park 51 mosque dispute in 2010 which erupted following the planning meeting in New York City to approve an Islamic community center within blocks of the World Trade Center site. In all three cases there was a spike followed by a decline in incidents. One might also notice that hate crime incidents in 2018 are much higher than in 2004 or 2013 indicating that the overall trend is upward.

One caveat about the FBI hate crime statistics is the likelihood of unreported incidents or the classification of a hate crime as something else. Reporting a hate crime against a Muslim is likely inhibited by institutional Islamophobia. The most high-profile example of this was the denial of a Federal hate crime

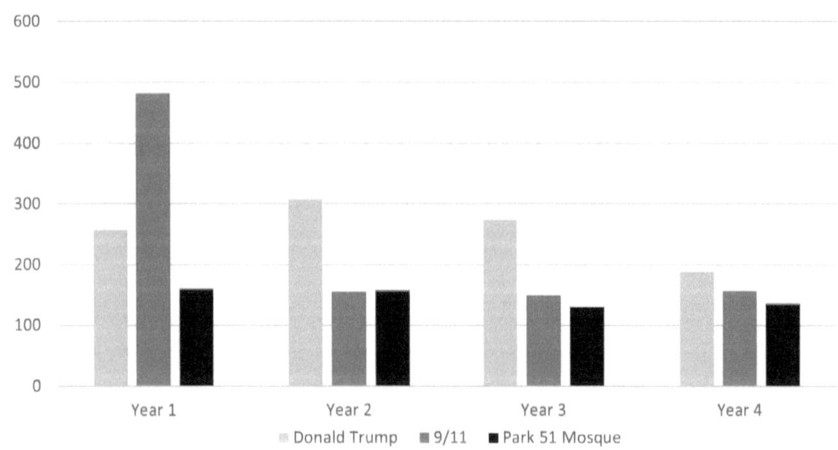

Figure 2.2 Hate Crime Incidents against Muslims in United States. Data compiled from The Uniform Crime Report at the Federal Bureau of Investigation.

charge in the murder of three Muslim students in 2015 in Chapel Hill, North Carolina by Craig Hicks, who had previously made Islamophobic comments on social media. At his sentencing Suzanne Barakat, the sister of one of the victims, revealed this bias by saying, "Somehow, when a white man commits gruesome acts of violence, he's a lone wolf, mentally deranged, or driven by a parking dispute."[45] Dr. Mohammad Abu-Salha, the father of one of the victims, was invited before Congress to discuss this increase in hate crimes, but was instead attacked for his Islamic identity.[46]

The institutional Islamophobia that might contribute to downward estimates in hate crimes against Muslims is evident in how the FBI has interacted with the American Muslim community. They have been surveilling this community since the late 1960s.[47] Following 9/11 there emerged a discourse that Muslims do not deserve the same rights as other people. Therefore, Muslims have been disproportionately targeted by counter-terrorism policies with material support claims, undercover informants and false statements in order to convict them on terrorism charges.[48] In this environment, it would be understandable if an American Muslim would not want to report a hate crime for fear of becoming entangled with the FBI.

The second reason identified by Penning for negative views of the Muslim community is religious beliefs.[49] This finding is connected to the findings of Hewstone et al.[50] Over the years conservative Christians have grown in their opposition to Islam and the American Muslim community. They have increasingly seen support for this community in alignment with the political left making Islam a partisan issue. It is for this reason that most Muslims have shifted away from the Republican Party when they had previously supported it.[51] In consequence, Uddin wrote, "it should come as no surprise then that many American Muslims have in recent years refused to support conservative Christians in their religious claims against abortion, contraception and same-sex marriage."[52]

The third reason identified by Penning for negative views toward Muslims is experience and education. The more experience people have with the American Muslim community and the more educated they are the less prejudiced they are toward them.[53] The literature on intergroup contact supports these findings. For example, Schmid, Hewstone and Al Ramiah found that more diverse areas in the United Kingdom encouraged more positive contact with Muslims.[54] Intuitively, the more that people know about the American Muslim community either through experience or education the less prejudice they feel toward them.

The problem is that there is a widely held belief that Muslims are militant fundamentalists.[55] This belief increases anxiety toward this community so that people avoid it. The amount of contact with Muslims in the United States is very low. According to the Public Religion Research Institute, only six percent of Americans say they have a conversation with a Muslim once a day.[56] The Muslim community largely remains a mystery for most Americans. For this reason, when Muslim rights are discussed they are often seen through the prism of national security.[57] They are guilty until proven innocent. As already discussed, this is institutional Islamophobia which creates bias in the system toward Muslims.

Even when discrimination is recognized within this context it is discussed as a potential national security issue. One example of this can be found in the recent book by Noah Rothman. In the book, Rothman criticized identity politics on both the political Right and Left. In a lengthy rebuke he criticized the prominent American Muslim political activist, Linda Sarsour, but later criticized the rise of Islamophobic discourse in the political Right. His reason for this criticism is that it created an isolated and dangerous community of Muslims. Rothman explained, "by alienating and stereotyping the American Muslims who are intent on assimilation, they risk encouraging the development of dangerous and isolated communities."[58] There are two assumptions here that are problematic. First, there is the assumption that American Muslims are interested in assimilating, which would be the loss of their Islamic identity in all but name only. Certainly, some Muslims have done this and will do this in the future, but not all. Second, it is assumed that anything short of assimilation leads to the development of "dangerous and isolated communities." If American Muslims wear Islamic clothing, use Islamic mannerisms, and pray five times a day then this is evidence of a lack of assimilation which is dangerous for some people.

Discrimination against Muslims is also dismissed as a natural byproduct of Muslim misdeeds or disputed all together. An example of this in academia is the article written by Akbaba and Fox. In 2011, Akbaba and Fox published an article that argued prejudice against Muslims in the West was not any more prevalent then prejudice toward other groups. The authors did not stop there. They found further that by comparison Christians suffered more in Muslim-majority countries. They then made a startling reference to the Golden Rule in an academic article. They wrote, "when comparing the treatment of Muslims in Christian-majority states to the treatment of Christians in Muslim-majority states—a comparison which has considerable normative implications on the basis of do unto others as you would have them do unto you."[59] This implies that because they found in their very limited analysis that Christians were more discriminated against in Muslim-majority countries that it made normative sense for Muslims to be more discriminated against in Christian-majority countries. If this is the case, then they deserve it. Therefore, the rights of Muslims in the United States should be directly linked to the rights of Christians in Muslim countries as if the United States retroactively awards rights to others. This also assumes that Muslims are a homogenous block who approve of religious persecution against other religious groups in Muslim-majority countries. American Muslims who immigrated to the United States and elsewhere left these countries because of their lack of rights. Think of the case of Saleh at the beginning of this chapter. In 2015, when Akbaba and Fox found that discrimination against Muslims was higher than other religious groups in the West they dismissed it again as the product of "securitization."[60]

The political left in the United States has recognized the reality of Muslims as an oppressed minority. However, the dichotomy of "good Muslim" versus "bad Muslim" is still part of their vocabulary. Uddin decried this as the championing of Muslim rights through the lens of patriotism.[61] The patriotism of Muslims is questioned and the support of Muslims is conditioned on them being patriotic or seen as patriotic. The image of the Muslim woman wearing an American flag hijab is an example of this.

It is not difficult to see with these varying perspectives on Islam and the Muslim community in the United States and a coalescing of these perspectives around a perception of a threat that there is support for anti-Sharia laws. The hypocrisy of championing religious liberty while legislating religious restrictions on Muslims is lost when Islam is cast as a dangerous and destabilizing force. The crowd that barged into the courthouse in Murfreesboro harbored these views as they felt no shame in saying them. The subsequent court case tried to legitimize them.

The next chapters of this book will look at each of the major factors explaining possible support for anti-Sharia legislation starting with what are seen as the major proponents of these laws and spreading narratives of Muslims and Islam as threats, the anti-Muslim groups.

NOTES

1. Sbenaty, Saleh, Personal communication (October 27, 2020).
2. Ibid.
3. Steinback, Robert. 2011. Jihad Against Islam. Montgomery, Alabama: Southern Poverty Law Center, 2011, https://www.splcenter.org/fighting-hate/intelligence-report/2011/jihad-against-islam.
4. Sbenaty, personal communication.
5. GhaneaBassiri, Kambiz. 2010. *A History of Islam in America: From the New World to the New World Order.* Cambridge: Cambridge University Press.
6. Ibid.
7. Ibid.
8. Schumann, Christoph. 2007. "A Muslim 'Diaspora' in the United States?" *The Muslim World* 97, no. 1, 11–32.
9. GhaneaBassiri, *A History of Islam in America.*
10. See the Association of Religion Data Archives here: http://www.thearda.com/.

11. Peek, Lori. 2005. "Becoming Muslim: The Development of a Religious Identity." *Sociology of Religion 66*, no. 3, 215.

12. O'Brien, John. 2011. "Spoiled Group Identities and Backstage Work." *Social Psychology Quarterly 74*, no. 3, 291–309.

13. Mohammed, Shaheed N. 2015. "The Muslims Next Door: Transgressive Hybridity in TLC'sAll-American Muslim." *Mass Communication and Society 18*, no. 1, 97–118.

14. Cesari, Jocelyne. 2011. "'Islamophobia' in the West: A Comparison Between Europe and America." In *Islamophobia: The Challenge of Pluralism in the 21st Century*, edited by John L. Esposito and Ibrahim Kalin, 21–43.

15. Skenderovic, Damir, and Christina Späti. 2019. "From Orientalism to Islamophobia: Reflections, Confirmations, and Reservations." *ReOrient* 4, no. 2, 130–143.

16. Ibid. 134.

17. Haque, Afshana, Carolyn Y. Tubbs, Emily P. Kahumoku-Fessler, and Matthew D. Brown. 2018. "Microaggressions and Islamophobia: Experiences of Muslims Across the United States and Clinical Implications." *Journal of Marital and Family Therapy* 45, no. 1, 76–91.

18. Ali, Yaser. 2012. "Shariah and Citizenship—How Islamophobia Is Creating a Second-Class Citizenry in America." *California Law Review 100*, no. 4, 1027–1068.

19. Kalmar, Ivan. 2019. "The Jew and the Odalisque: Two Tropes Lost on the Way from Classic Orientalism to Islamophobia." *ReOrient* 4, no. 2, 181–196.

20. Uddin, Asma T. 2019. *When Islam Is Not a Religion: Inside America's Fight for Religious Freedom*. New York: Simon & Schuster.

21. Taleb, Nassim N. 2018. *Skin in the Game: Hidden Asymmetries in Daily Life*. New York: Random House.

22. Wood, Graeme. "What ISIS Really Wants." *The Atlantic*, March 2015. https://www.theatlantic.com/magazine/archive/2015/03/what-isis-really-wants/384980/.

23. Allen, Chris. 2010. *Islamophobia*. New York: Routledge.

24. Ibid.

25. Ibid.

26. Garner, Steve, and Saher Selod. 2014. "The Racialization of Muslims: Empirical Studies of Islamophobia." *Critical Sociology 41,* no. 1, 9–19.

27. Love, Erik. 2009. "Confronting Islamophobia in the United States: framing civil rights activism among Middle Eastern Americans." *Patterns of Prejudice 43*, no. 3–4, 401–425.

28. Garner & Selod, *The Racialization of Muslims.*

29. Ibid., 17.

30. Hewstone, Miles, Abigail Clare, Anna Newheiser, and Alberto Voci. 2011. "Making and unmaking prejudice: Religious affiliation reduces the impact of mortality salience on intergroup attitudes." *PsycEXTRA Dataset 18*, no. 3, 143–155.

31. Love, *Confronting Islamophobia in the United States.*

32. Bail, Christopher A. 2016. *Terrified: How Anti-Muslim Fringe Organizations Became Mainstream*. Princeton: Princeton University Press.

33. Khan, Saeed A. 2012. "Sharia Law, Islamophobia and the U.S. Constitution: New Tectonic Plates of the Culture Wars." *University of Maryland Law Journal of Race, Religion, Gender and Class* 12, no. 1, 124.

34. Ibid.

35. Bail, *Terrified.*

36. Ibid.

37. Kalkan, Kerem O., Geoffrey C. Layman, and John C. Green. 2018. "Will Americans Vote for Muslims? Cultural Outgroup Antipathy, Candidate Religion, and U.S. Voting Behavior." *Politics and Religion* 11, no. 4, 798–829.

38. Petrzelka, Peggy, and Paul Jacobs. 2016. "Why Utah? The "Reddest of Red States" and inclusive immigration reform." *The Social Science Journal 53*, no. 2, 156–166.

39. Uddin, *When Islam Is Not a Religion.*

40. Penning, James M. 2009. "Americans' Views of Muslims and Mormons: A Social Identity Theory Approach." *Politics and Religion 2*, no. 2, 277–302.

41. Cesari, *'Islamophobia' in the West.*

42. Yin, Tung. 2013. "Were Timothy McVeigh and the Unabomber the only White Terrorists?: Race, Religion, and the Perception of Terrorism." *Alabama Civil Rights & Civil Liberties Law Review 4*, 33–87.

43. Uddin, *When Islam Is Not a Religion.*

44. FBI hate crime statistics can be found here: https://ucr.fbi.gov/hate-crime.

45. Quote can be found here: https://www.wunc.org/post/police-apologize-chapel-hill-shooting-victims-families-0.

46. An analysis on this meeting can be found here: https://qz.com/1590890/a-hate-crime-hearing-shows-the-end-of-decency-in-us-politics/.

47. GhaneaBassiri, Kambiz. 2010. *A History of Islam in America: From the New World to the New World Order.* Cambridge: Cambridge University Press.

48. Ahmed, Sameer. 2017. "Is history repeating itself? Sentencing young American Muslims in the War on Terror." *The Yale Law Journal 126*, no. 5, 1242–1599.

49. Penning, *Americans' Views of Muslims and Mormons.*

50. Hewstone et al., *Making and Unmaking Prejudice.*

51. Ayers, John W. 2007. "Changing Sides: 9/11 and the American Muslim Voter." *Review of Religious Research 49*, no. 2, 187–198.; Pervez, Fouad, and Dalia Mogahed. 2016. *American Muslim Poll: Participation, Priorities, and Facing Prejudice in the 2016 Election.* Washington, DC: Institute of Social Policy and Understanding, https://www.ispu.org/wp-content/uploads/2016/08/poll2016-1.pdf.

52. Uddin, *When Islam Is Not a Religion*, 299.

53. Penning, *Americans' Views of Muslims and Mormons.*

54. Schmid, Katharina, Ananthi A. Ramiah, and Miles Hewstone. 2014. "Neighborhood Ethnic Diversity and Trust." *Psychological Science 25*, no. 3, 665–674.

55. Gottschalk, Peter, and Gabriel Greenberg. 2008. *Islamophobia: Making Muslims the Enemy.* Lanham: Rowman & Littlefield.

56. See a summary of this research here: https://www.prri.org/spotlight/fact-sheet-american-attitudes-on-muslims/.

57. Uddin, *When Islam Is Not a Religion.*

58. Rothman, Noah. 2019. *Unjust: Social Justice and the Unmaking of America.* New York: Simon & Schuster, 88.

59. Akbaba, Yasemin, and Jonathan Fox. 2011. "Religious Discrimination against Muslim Minorities in Christian Majority Countries: A Unique Case?" *Politics, Religion & Ideology 12*, no. 4, 467.

60. Fox, Jonathan, and Yasemin Akbaba. 2015. "Securitization of Islam and religious discrimination: Religious minorities in Western democracies, 1990–2008." *Comparative European Politics 13*, no. 2, 175–197.

61. Uddin, *When Islam Is Not a Religion.*

Chapter 3

Anti-Muslim Groups

Hate groups are one of those quirks of free and democratic societies with varying levels of activity dependent on the laws of those nations. In the United States, the freedom of speech and assembly enshrined in the Constitution have granted these groups the freedom to spread their ideology through websites and in the streets as they rally others to their cause. Although most of these groups claim they are non-violent proponents of their cause, the threat of violence is never far beneath the surface for these groups.

The link between hate group activity and hate crimes has not been established in the literature.[1] Still, the motivation to commit a hate crime is never clear while hate groups often provide the motivation through their dehumanization of whole groups of people. Dharmapala and McAdams assessed the possible linkages between hate speech and hate crime and argued that based on esteem theory those most likely to commit hate crimes overestimate the number of those that approve of those crimes which is made worse by the barrage of hate speech coming from hate groups.[2]

Hate groups have always targeted racial and religious minorities. African Americans have faced the brunt of these groups followed by Jews. Increasingly, these groups have targeted the Muslim community. This increase has been so pronounced that the Southern Poverty Law Center which tracks hate groups had to create a separate category for these groups. Some of them have already been mentioned in this book such as ACT! for America.

When taken together with other groups that have anti-Muslim agendas although not the core of their mission there are some states that have more anti-Muslim hate group activity. In 2010, California had the most followed by Texas, Florida, Mississippi, and New Jersey. It is probably not a coincidence that of those top five states, three have anti-Sharia laws. Compare this to Hawaii and Alaska that had no anti-Muslim hate groups in 2010 followed in increasing order by Vermont, South Dakota and Rhode Island. Of these states only one (South Dakota) has an anti-Sharia law. See figure 3.1.

According to the Othering and Belonging Institute at the University of California Berkeley, a number of these hate groups have promoted these laws across the United States. Besides ACT! for America, the American Public Policy Alliance, the Florida Family Association, Florida Family Policy Council, Christian Family Coalition, the Center for Security Policy, Stop the Islamization of America, and the Home School Legal Defense Association have all advocated for these bills in different states. The biggest players are ACT! for America and the American Public Policy Alliance. They have been involved in almost all the anti-Sharia laws proposed and passed in state legislatures across the country.

Their involvement is known because many of the bills introduced follow the model legislation designed by these groups. This legislation is promoted at their events and on their websites and social media accounts. They also meet with state legislators many of whom become the bill sponsors. They capitalize on ignorance on Islam and the Muslim community by spreading fear of a "silent jihad" or an effort to take over the government by Islamists with Sharia as their tool.

Hate groups such as these have been associated with such phenomenon as social identity and social dominance. According to social identity theory, people naturally create in-groups and out-groups.[3] This helps in the internal consolidation of the in-group through established expectations and behavior that is often juxtaposed to the out-group. Members of the out-group are simply "not like us." This gives rise to prejudice toward the out-group that is

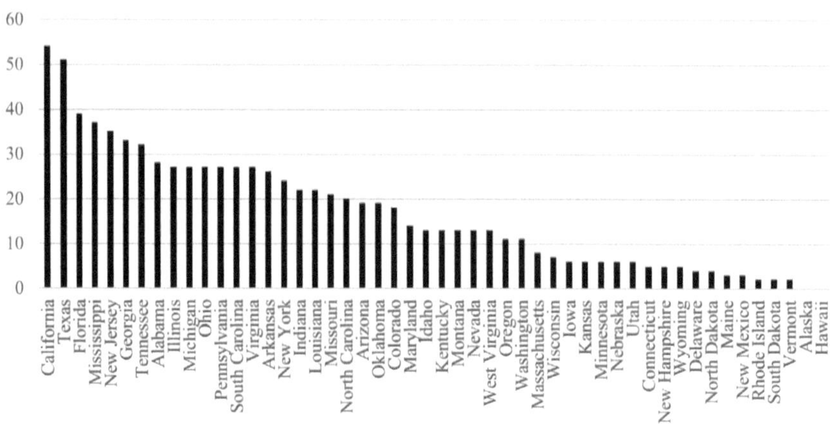

Figure 3.1 Number of Anti-Muslim Hate Groups by State (2010). Data from the Southern Poverty Law Center.

attenuated through group conflict over perceived and actual loss of power or access to resources.

These groups can form along religious or racial lines, which is often the case especially as it comes to defining Muslims as an out-group. Even if the divider is not clear, the minimal group paradigm argues that simply telling people that they are part of a group is all that is needed to create group dynamics as previously described. This is where hate groups might make their biggest impact. By arguing that the United States is a Judeo-Christian nation that is being threatened by an outside Islamic force, those that identify with that tradition may form an in-group around that tradition in response to a perceived Islamic threat.

Hate groups celebrate the in-group which aids in group esteem. Group esteem contributes to personal esteem. This may explain why there is a lukewarm response to White nationalist groups in the United States. The dominant racial and religious group feels less threatened by White nationalists, Christian identitarians, and anti-Muslim groups because these groups celebrate their identity. This contributes to the frustration over approaches to national security that target racial and religious minorities while ignoring equal or greater threats from groups that represent the dominant racial and religious group.

Hate groups are particularly effective at degrading out-groups and capitalizing on what is known as fear-extinction bias. Fear-extinction bias is conditioned fear toward a particular group that signals danger.[4] Fear toward an out-group is particularly potent in which images of turbaned or masked men holding Kalashnikovs are accompanied by messages of an Islamic invasion and the imposition of Sharia where women will be promptly placed under a burqa and public executions will make the streets run red with blood.

It's fear and the accompanying anxiety that are most important for maintaining out-group animus. In research on inter-group dynamics, there is an argument that through greater contact between members of the in-group and out-group prejudice can be reduced with greater community cohesion.[5] More recent research has concluded that several mediators intervene in that relationship. One of those mediators is the level of anxiety or perceived threat of the out-group.[6] If the interaction can reduce anxiety, then this will go a long way in reducing prejudice experienced toward the out-group. Hate groups work to ensure that anxiety toward this out-group remains high.

The example of Linda Sarsour is particularly poignant here. Sarsour has worked as a community activist in Brooklyn most of her adult life. She is a Muslim and of Palestinian descent. She is most prominently known today as one of the co-chairs of the Women's March in 2017 in Washington, DC, following the inauguration of Donald Trump. As she has gained prominence, the attacks against her have intensified. She observed that millions have been spent to discredit and defame her by linking her with terrorist movements in the Middle East and claiming that she supports the imposition of Sharia in the United States.[7] This is all meant to scare others from her and prevent her from having a platform. At the core of these efforts one will find the anti-Muslim hate groups many of which are lobbying for the passage of anti-Sharia laws.

Inter-group contact is also limited by group salience. If quality contact occurs between a member of the in-group and out-group, then will that experience come to define the group as a whole?[8] Unfortunately, there seems to be a tendency to define Muslims as "good" and "bad" as previously discussed in chapter 2. This means that a good interaction may lead one to conclude that their interaction was with one of the "good Muslims." Further, anti-Muslim groups have worked to create distrust even in these interactions by arguing that a fundamental aspect of Islam is something known as Taqiyya. Taqiyya is the, "permission to dissimulate, and even deny one's faith in times of personal danger" in Islam.[9] The term and practice is nuanced and rarely interpreted in the way argued by these groups. As explained by Mariuma, "as opposed to learned arguments among Muslim scholars, the non-Muslim writers who use Taqiyya as a form of Islamophobic polemic attack are actually quite crude, but struggle toward the same vision of convincing the reader that statements by Muslims about harmony and 'fitting in' are false."[10]

This messaging by the anti-Muslim hate groups has only grown in prominence over the years as explained by Christopher Bail in his book, "Terrified: How Anti-Muslim Fringe Organizations Became Mainstream."[11] In this book, Bail described the growing influence of these hate groups on the media and increasing connections between these groups and mainstream organizations. As explained by Bail with a focus on the period between 2001 and 2008, "this period was characterized by an increase in concern among conservative and center-right civil society organizations about the rise of Shari'ah or Islamic law within the United States."[12] It is almost as if an antipathy toward Sharia united these groups and linked them with mainstream organizations.

Of these mainstream organizations, Bail mentioned the Anti-Defamation League (ADL). It should be noted that the ADL has opposed anti-Sharia laws because of their possible usage against halakhah. In some cases, halakhah was included in a list of so-called foreign laws. When describing her efforts to lobby against the Florida law, Laila noted that the ADL was an ally in that fight.[13]

Based on the growing prominence of these groups and the mainstreaming of their message, any study of the proliferation of anti-Sharia laws would need to include their activities. A variable measuring the size of their presence in the state is included in the analysis in this book. This is described in more detail in chapter 9.

NOTES

1. Ryan, Mark E., and Peter T. Leeson. 2011. "Hate groups and hate crime." *International Review of Law and Economics* 31, no. 4, 256–262.

2. Dharmapala, Dhammika and McAdams, Richard H., "Words that Kill? Economic Perspectives on Hate Speech and Hate Crimes" (2003). Economics Working Papers. 200305. https://opencommons.uconn.edu/econ_wpapers/200305.

3. Cuhadar, Esra, and Bruce Dayton. 2011. "The Social Psychology of Identity and Inter-group Conflict: From Theory to Practice." *International Studies Perspectives* 12, no. 3, 273–293.

4. Navarrete, Carlos D., Andreas Olsson, Arnold K. Ho, Wendy B. Mendes, Lotte Thomsen, and James Sidanius. 2009. "Fear Extinction to an Out-Group Face: The Role of Target Gender." *Psychological Science* 20, no. 2, 155–158.

5. Allport, Gordon W. 1954. *The Nature of Prejudice*. Cambridge, MA: Addison-Wesley Pub. Co.

6. Pettigrew, Thomas F., and Linda R. Tropp. 2008. "How Does Intergroup Contact Reduce Prejudice? Meta-Analytic Tests of Three Mediators." *European Journal of Social Psychology* 38, no. 6, 922-934.

7. Sarsour, Linda. 2020 *We Are Not Here to Be Bystanders: A Memoir of Love and Resistance*. New York: 37 Ink.

8. Tredoux, Colin, and Gillian Finchilescu. 2007. "The Contact Hypothesis and Intergroup Relations 50 Years on: Introduction to the Special Issue." *South African Journal of Psychology* 37, no. 4, 667–678.

9. Mariuma, Yarden. 2014. "Taqiyya as Polemic, Law and Knowledge: Following an Islamic Legal Term through the Worlds of Islamic Scholars, Ethnographers, Polemicists and Military Men." *The Muslim World* 104, no. 1–2, 91.

10. Ibid. 98–99.

11. Bail, Christopher A. 2016. *Terrified: How Anti-Muslim Fringe Organizations Became Mainstream*. Princeton: Princeton University Press.

12. Ibid. 72.

13. Abdelaziz, Laila, personal communication, October 27, 2020.

Chapter 4

Muslim Presence and Evangelicalism

The presence of Muslims has been considered a trigger for anti-Muslim activities. I published an article several years ago when I was still a doctoral student that found significant differences in the number of hate groups in states that had high numbers of mosque controversies versus states that had no mosque controversies. My argument at the time was rooted in the social dominance theory and a social dominance orientation that led to the rise of hate groups.[1] The analysis was rudimentary and did not consider causality. Years later as my methodological rigor improved, I published another paper that assessed the causal relationship between the size of the Muslim population and the presence of hate groups in a state. The result was nonsignificant.[2]

The relationship between the size of the Muslim population and anti-Muslim movements is not clear just like the relationship between hate speech and hate crime is not clear. In addition, anti-Muslim movements are not homogeneous in their membership or platform. As argued in the last chapter, there are efforts by these groups to drive the narrative around Islam and Muslims, but one cannot ignore the presence of general antipathy toward the religion. Mosque protests are examples of this. Although there are clear examples where anti-Muslim groups generated and accelerated protests around proposed mosques, most mosque protests started rather organically within individual communities.

An example of this is cited in my original paper on the topic in Palos Heights, Illinois. This mosque controversy pre-dated the 9/11 terror attacks showing that these attacks only amplified anti-Muslim sentiment.[3] Between 2010 and 2012, the State of Illinois had more mosque disputes than any other state. Practically all of these disputes occurred in the Chicago metropolitan area. One example ended in a successful court case litigated by the Muslim Legal Defense Fund (*Islamic Center of Western Suburbs* v. *County of*

DuPage).[4] The mosque had sought conversion of a vacant house into a mosque in 2008. There was resistance over the proposed project because of zoning restrictions that required the mosque leadership to file for an appeal. At some point during the process the county development committee voted to approve the project which sent it to the county board for a final vote. The board voted against it. After years of litigation the mosque finally opened for daily prayers in 2015. That is seven years of delay (and considerable expense) for a Muslim community to enjoy the same constitutionally protected rights as other communities.

It is interesting though that despite there being so many mosque protests in Illinois, not a single anti-Sharia law was introduced into the state legislature. Even today, Illinois does not have an anti-Sharia law and is very unlikely to have one. See figure 4.1. As one can see in this figure, there were more protests in Illinois, California, and New York than other states. It is not coincidental that these states also have higher concentrations of Muslims with New York, Illinois and California in the top four states by Muslim population. See figure 2.1. Larger Muslim populations necessitate more mosques and the proposal of more mosques leads to more mosque protests. This connection is pretty clear, but what is interesting in these three states is that between 2010 and 2012 not a single anti-Sharia law was introduced or passed. Only New Jersey which had four controversies over mosques introduced anti-Sharia legislation.

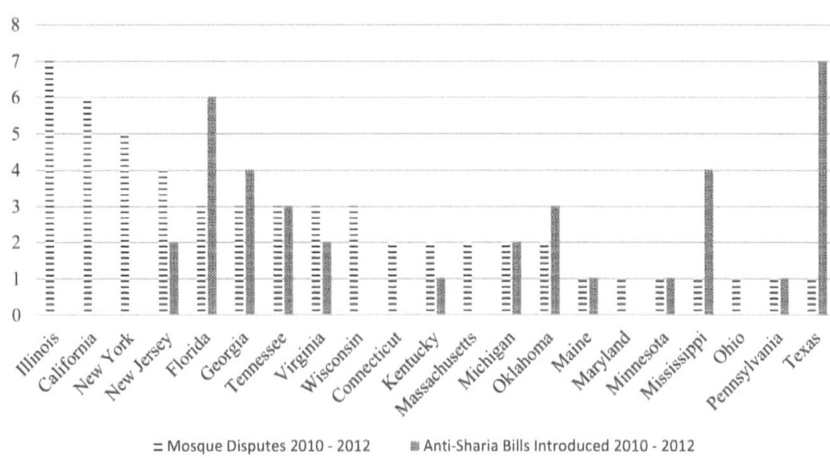

Figure 4.1 Mosque Disputes and Anti-Sharia Laws by State (2010–2012). Data compiled from Pew Center for Religion & Public Life (mosque disputes); Southern Poverty Law Center and Othering and Belonging Institute at University of California–Berkeley (anti-Sharia laws).

Further, Texas, which has the largest population of Muslims of any state, only had one mosque dispute between 2010 and 2012, while it introduced anti-Sharia legislation seven times in this time period. The legislators in Texas were intent on passing this law and they were successful in doing it. One would imagine that Texas would have more mosque projects given the size of the Muslim population there and therefore there would be more mosque protests. This was not the case. At the local level, Muslims are treated fairly well in the State of Texas while the state legislators work to disparage the community.

The only states that had concordantly high levels of mosque disputes and anti-Sharia law introductions were the states of Florida, Georgia, and Tennessee. These states, but especially Florida and Tennessee, present examples of where anti-Muslim fervor is particularly high and manifesting at both the local and state level. Florida and Tennessee both have anti-Sharia laws. Florida has a larger population of Muslims, but not even in the top five states by Muslim population. Tennessee has a very small population of Muslims. Given this, it is not likely that the size of the Muslim population is spurring anti-Muslim activity alone.

CONTACT AND SOCIAL DOMINANCE

Those that theorize that increased contact between in-groups and out-groups reduces prejudice also understand that there are many conditions that can influence this result. Cuhadar and Dayton identified several of these conditions. They argued that there needs to be equal status between the groups in which there are still common goals. The groups have to be interdependent that allow some level of quality interaction that is supported by group norms. This contact also needs to be facilitated by governing bodies and institutions.[5] It is unlikely that these conditions exist with the Muslim community and it certainly is not supported by the governing bodies and institutions especially if they are voting down mosque projects and supporting anti-Sharia laws.

Instead, there are several mediators that prevent any quality contact to occur that will lead to reduced prejudice. As discussed in chapter 3, one of these mediators is anxiety toward the out-group. Efforts to scare people about Islam are a major influence and this is where hate groups gain their greatest audience. Other mediators are social attitudes. John Duckitt developed the concept of dual-process motivation in which there were two related, but also distinct ideologies.[6] Right-wing authoritarianism manifests prejudice that is linked with a real or perceived threat. Fear and anxiety made worse by uncertainty fuel this ideological orientation. It has been found that those harboring these views see their prejudice reduce toward a threatening outsider through intergroup contact.[7]

The other ideology is social dominance. Social dominance is about competition particularly between high status groups and low status groups.[8] High status groups fear the loss of status and the rise of low status groups. It is zero-sum in which any gains made by the low status groups are seen as losses to the high status group. The goal is the maintenance of the status quo. Those that possess this view are less convinced through intergroup contact in which this contact may actually increase their social dominance orientation and thereby their levels of prejudice toward the out-group.[9]

There was an interesting study done on the attitudes of White Americans in which the authors conducted an experiment where they split respondents to a survey that assessed pro-White bias. Half of the respondents simply took the survey without any intervention (the control group) and the other half were first subjected to information that by 2042 based on demographic estimates the United States will be a majority-minority nation that is the majority of people will be who we consider minorities today. The authors found that those that were subjected to this information had a higher pro-White bias than those that did not read it. The authors explained that this was evidence of perceived threats from the increasing size of the minority population.[10] Although the authors did not discuss social dominance, this is a perfect example of a rise in a social dominance orientation.

One can imagine this threat arising because of the differences in race between the majority of Muslims and the majority of Christians, who are White in the United States. Given that the United States is a particularly religious nation, it would make more sense to think of this within religious terms. Religious fundamentalism and its social dominance orientation are present across all faith communities including Muslims. This is the idea that one's religion should dominate all other forms of religion and the rise of one of these competing religions is seen as a direct threat to that dominance. It is very common to call out "Islamic supremacy" such as its manifestations in movements like the Islamic State of Iraq and Syria (ISIS), but rare to do so for other faith communities. One religious movement in the United States that has increasingly been associated with Christian fundamentalism is Evangelical Christianity.

EVANGELICALS AND ISLAM

Evangelicals have been a part of the story of the United States since the beginning. They argued for the separation of government from religion in so far as it would keep government out of religion. This separated them from the

Puritans, who felt that government and religion should be joined. Ultimately, the arguments of the Evangelicals prevailed and the United States not only granted Free Exercise, but Non-Establishment as well.[11]

There were likely good reasons that the Evangelicals took this position. They believe in the authority of the Old and New Testaments of the Bible. As it says in the New Testament, "No one can serve two masters."[12] For them, the rules/regulations and morals/values outlined in the Bible are very important.[13] If the actions of government deviate from these rules or morals, then those in the Evangelical community would prefer if the government keeps its distance. Given the unlikelihood that the United States would establish a theocracy based on the Bible, the natural inclination is for the government to remain aloof as to the affairs of religious communities.

One can argue that this strand of thought is still very prominent in Evangelical circles. Today, there are three sub-groups of Evangelical Christianity. There are the Pentecostal/Charismatic and Neo-Evangelical variants, which can be likened to the older versions of evangelicalism in the United States. The third group is the Fundamentalist variant. This form of evangelicalism has become more involved in the affairs of the government in ways that are more closely aligned with the Puritans. In this way, this form of evangelicalism is different from its traditional roots. It also happens that Fundamentalist Evangelicals are vehemently anti-Muslim.[14]

In one of the rare studies on the anti-Sharia laws, Mitchell and Toner studied the passage of these laws by the states and found the size of the Evangelical Christian community predicted their passage. Their results confirmed a general problem of Islamophobia in the Evangelical community.[15] Further, Chouhoud and Mogahed found in a study of Islamophobia between different faith communities that White Evangelicals scored the highest in most measures of prejudice toward Muslims.[16]

It is likely that Muslims are seen as an amoral and deviant group by Fundamentalist Evangelicals. For them, banning Sharia or any other Islamic practice no matter how unconstitutional is a moral imperative. Some Evangelicals see Islam as a contaminant.[17] There are certainly plenty of examples of this perspective openly voiced by leaders of this community. Following the 9/11 terror attacks and after President George W. Bush tried to argue that Islam was a peaceful religion, many Evangelical leaders, who had supported Bush because of his own Evangelical beliefs, disagreed with him. Jerry Falwell described Muhammad, the Prophet of Islam, as a terrorist while Jerry Vines described him as demon-possessed. Franklin Graham, son of Billy Graham, described Islam as evil.[18] Many Evangelicals rallied around the notion that following the 9/11 terror attacks that the United States was engaged in a civilizational battle against Islam.

This is not a view held by all Evangelicals, but are held most likely by Fundamentalist Evangelicals. As discussed in the previous section, fundamentalism is rooted in a social dominance perspective. Based on this perspective, it may be more likely that as the proportion of Muslims increase in a state that prejudice toward them would increase among Evangelicals. If the Evangelical population is large enough it could influence legislators in the state to propose and adopt an anti-Sharia law.

A simple correlation between the percentage Muslim and the percentage Evangelical in a state was not significant. This religion census was done last time in 2010. As can be seen in table 4.1, the correlation coefficient is quite low meaning that there is almost no relationship between the sizes of the two populations. This does not support the notion that the increased presence of Muslims in a state is activating a social dominance perspective.

However, the percentage Evangelical was significantly correlated with the number of anti-Sharia laws introduced in a state. As this percentage increased, the number of anti-Sharia laws introduced increased along with it. This tentatively confirms the research of Mitchell and Toner. The empirical connection would then be with the size of the Evangelical community which is not dependent on the size of the Muslim community.

This is an interesting connection which may be rooted in the effects of narratives around Islam and Muslims possibly perpetuated by hate groups and in general discourse. If it is an accurate assessment that among Evangelicals are those of the Fundamentalist branch and those that adhere to this have a social dominance orientation, then it would make sense that social dominance messages generated by hate groups resonate with this group. An anti-Sharia law would have a receptive audience among Evangelicals who would demand legislative action.

The relationship can be seen graphically in figure 4.2. When the states are organized from greatest to least based on the proportion of the state that is Evangelical, a definable downward trend can be seen with the

Table 4.1 Ranked Correlation of Muslims, Evangelicals, Mosque Disputes, and Anti-Sharia Laws

	# of Mosque Disputes	*% Evangelical*
% Muslim	.676*	.017
# of Anti-Sharia Laws	.081	.485*

Note: Spearman's Rho; *p ≤ .01 (two-tailed); N = 50; # of Mosque Disputes (2010–2012) based on Pew data; % Evangelical and % Muslim (2010) based on data from the Association of Religion Data Archives; # of Anti-Sharia Laws (2010–2019) based on data from the Southern Poverty Law Center.

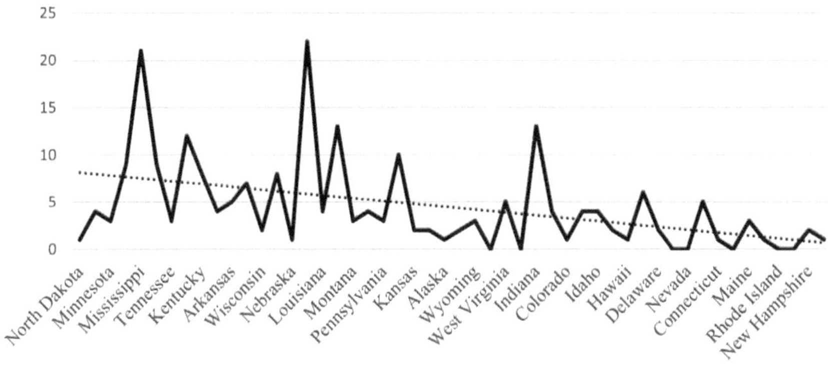

Figure 4.2 States from Greatest to Least Proportion Evangelical with Number of Anti-Sharia Laws Introduced (2010–2019). Data compiled from Pew Center for Religion & Public Life (mosque disputes); Southern Poverty Law Center and Othering and Belonging Institute at University of California--Berkeley (anti-Sharia laws).

number of anti-Sharia laws introduced in the states. This possible relationship cannot be ignored and it is included as a factor in the analysis in this book.

The proportion of Muslims in a state was not significantly correlated with the introduction of anti-Sharia laws as shown in table 4.1. Although this may mean that intergroup conflict is not an issue, it also means that intergroup contact may not matter either. Some states have large numbers of Muslims proportionally with only the introduction of a few anti-Sharia laws or none at all. Other states that have similarly large populations of Muslims have introduced the law many times and, in some cases, passed it. The evidence is inconclusive.

However, the proportion of Muslims in a state is very significantly correlated with the number of mosque disputes. As the number of Muslims increase in a state there is an increasing number of mosque projects. This increases the likelihood of a mosque dispute. Although the correlation is quite high, it is not perfect indicating that this is not the case in all states. Some states have a relatively high proportion of Muslims with relatively few mosque disputes while other states have a lower proportion of Muslims with more mosque disputes.

Despite its nonsignificance, it is still theoretically prudent to include a factor measuring the size of the Muslim population in an analysis on the introduction and passage of anti-Sharia laws. This factor has been included in the analysis in this book. The details of this analysis can be found in chapter 9.

NOTES

1. Hummel, Daniel. 2012. "Principles over Prejudice: Social Dominance Theory and the Mosques' Controversy in American Cities." *Journal of Muslim Minority Affairs* 32, no. 1, 32–46.

2. Hummel, Daniel. 2018. "Hate Groups and Muslim Population Changes in the Fifty States: Does the Presence of Muslims Encourage Hate Group Formation?" *International Journal on Minority and Group Rights* 25, no. 2, 317–332.

3. Hummel, *Principles over Prejudice.*

4. Hummel, Daniel. 2017. "Peace Profile: Muslim Legal Fund of America." *Peace Review* 29, no. 3, 401–407.

5. Cuhadar, Esra, and Bruce Dayton. 2011. "The Social Psychology of Identity and Inter-group Conflict: From Theory to Practice." *International Studies Perspectives* 12, no. 3, 273–293.

6. Duckitt, John. 2001. "A dual-process cognitive-motivational theory of ideology and prejudice." *Advances in Experimental Social Psychology* 33, 41–113.

7. Asbrock, Frank, Oliver Christ, John Duckitt, and Chris G. Sibley. 2011. "Differential Effects of Intergroup Contact for Authoritarians and Social Dominators." *Personality and Social Psychology Bulletin* 38, no. 4, 477–490.

8. Küpper, Beate, Carina Wolf, and Andreas Zick. 2010. "Social Status and Anti-Immigrant Attitudes in Europe: An Examination from the Perspective of Social Dominance Theory." *International Journal of Conflict and Violence* 4, no. 2, 205–219.

9. Asbrock et al., *Differential Effects of Intergroup Contact.*

10. Craig, Maureen A., and Jennifer A. Richeson. 2014. "On the Precipice of a "Majority-Minority" America." *Psychological Science* 25, no. 6, 1189–1197.

11. John Witte, Jr. 1999. *Religion And The American Constitutional Experiment: Essential Rights And Liberties*. Boulder, CO: Westview Press.

12. Found in Matthew 6:24.

13. McAllister-Wilson, David. 2016. Beyond cooties and crushes: The potential for evangelical leadership in Christian engagement with Islam. *Journal of Ecumenical Studies* 51 (2), 264–270.

14. Hoover, Dennis R. 2004. Is evangelicalism itching for a civilization fight?: A media study. *Brandywine Review of Faith & International Affairs* 2(1), 11–6.

15. Mitchell, Joshua L., and Brendan Toner. 2016. "Exploring the Foundations of US State-Level Anti-Sharia Initiatives." *Politics and Religion* 9, no. 4, 720–743.

16. Chouhoud, Youssef, and Dalia Mogahed. 2018. *American Muslim Poll 2018.* Washington, DC: Institute for Social Policy and Understanding. https://www.ispu.org/american-muslim-poll-2018-full-report/.

17. McAllister-Wilson, *Beyond Cooties and Crushes.*

18. Durham, Martin. 2004. Evangelical Protestantism and foreign policy in the united states after September 11. *Patterns of Prejudice* 38 (2), 145–158.

Chapter 5

Religiosity in the United States

It is necessary to consider religiosity as opposed to religion separately in an analysis on anti-Sharia laws. This assumes that those that follow a religion are not necessarily extremely religious. There are many reasons for following a religion or being involved with a religious community. Religiosity does not have to be one of the reasons.

Religiosity is basically religious salience or the importance of religion in one's life. Individuals that are more religious tend to attend more religious services, pray more or observe the edicts of their religion more closely. They are often derisively referred to as fundamentalists and dismissed as radicals. There is an apprehension toward them because it is assumed that they are not easy to be reasoned with even within one's own religious community. All of these assumptions are not necessarily true, but some have lived up to these assumptions.

Evangelical Christians are often assumed to be predominantly ultra-religious. Again, this is not necessarily the case. Those who refer to themselves as Evangelicals represent a multitude of different churches with different ideological orientations as explored in the last chapter. There is a fundamentalist branch, which tends to be more Islamophobic. Even with this branch the relationship between the size of the Evangelical community and the proportion of people that claim to be very religious is not a perfect match.

Gallup collects survey data on religiosity across the fifty states during most years. The survey asks about the importance of religion in one's life. The scale ranges from not very important to very important. The percentages for each category are comparable between the states. The percentage that indicate that religion is very important for them are considered the most religious. When comparing this data with the size of the Evangelical community (also by percentage in a state), it is not a perfect correlation. See table 5.1.

Table 5.1 Correlation with Size of Evangelical Population and Religiosity

	% Evangelical
% Very Religious	.652*

Note: N = 50 states. *p ≤ .01 (two-tailed). Data from the Association of Religion Data Archives (% Evangelical) and Gallup (% Very Religious).

Still, the correlation is quite high (scale of 0 to 1). Those states that tend to have a higher proportion of their populations that are very religious also tend to have a higher proportion of their populations that are Evangelical. Despite this possible connection, there is much variability between the states on religiosity as there are in many factors. Mississippi, Alabama, Utah, Louisiana, and South Carolina are the top five states in the country for the importance of religion. In Mississippi, slightly more than 60 percent of the population indicate that religion is very important to them. Compare this to Vermont where only 21 percent of the population claim to be that religious. See figure 5.1.

As can be seen in figure 5.1, there is much variability between the states on religiosity. The average is about 40 percent represented by the line in the graph. One might notice that there is a political division between those states that are above average and those states that are below average. Below average states tend to be more Democratically-controlled. Consider the electoral college results of the 2016 election. Of the 23 states below average on religiosity, 17 of them voted for Hillary Clinton, the Democratic candidate for President. Of the 22 states above the average, only 2 did not vote for Donald Trump, the Republican candidate.

Despite these divisions, one should not associate religiosity with the political Right entirely. Philip Jenkins explored the rise of the religious Left in his

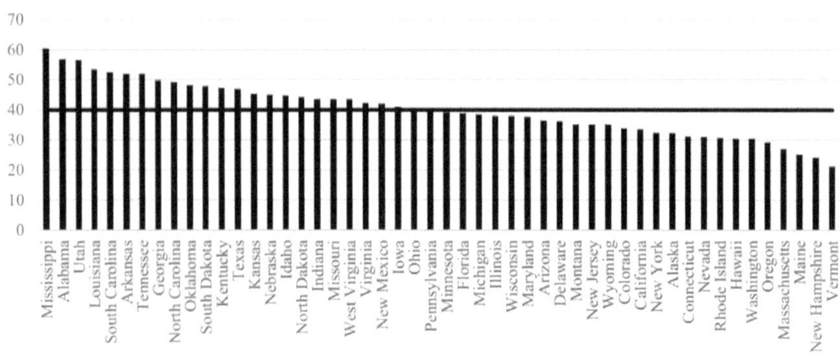

Figure 5.1 Average of Percent Very Religious by State (2012–2016). Data compiled from Gallup religion poll: https://news.gallup.com/poll/1690/religion.aspx.

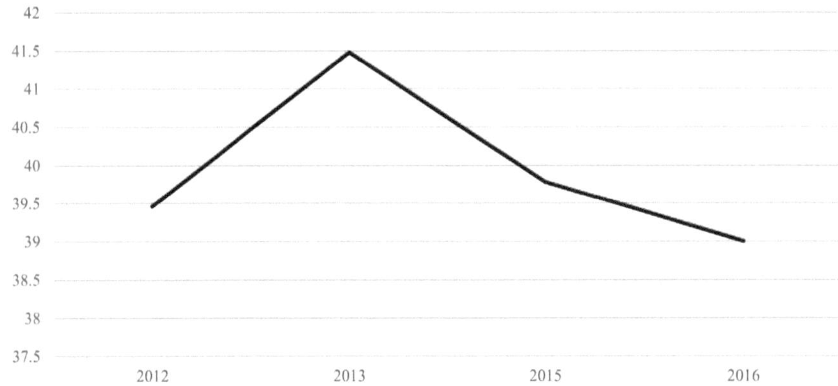

Figure 5.2 Change in Average Religiosity in the United States. Data compiled from Gallup religion poll: https://news.gallup.com/poll/1690/religion.aspx.

book *American Prophets: The Religious Roots of Progressive Politics and the Ongoing Fight for the Soul of the Country.*[1] In his book, Jenkins described the religious Left as the, "beating heart of modern progressivism."[2] He noted that historically, liberal Christianity was the most important form of religious expression in politics and that the fight against communism during the Cold War shifted this. Although he added that there has been an uncomfortable religious reawakening in the political Left, one cannot deny its importance in the Democratic Party especially when it comes to ascertaining electoral victories. He attributed the victories of President Obama to this connection.

It should also be noted that religiosity, in general, is declining across the United States. According to the Gallup data, religiosity peaked in 2013, but has been in decline since then. See figure 5.2. When considering more years, Gallup has data going back to 1992, when 58 percent of Americans stated that religion was very important to them in 1992. Compare this to 48 percent as of 2020.[3] Some observers have linked this to the declining religiosity of younger generations. It is a decline not only in religiosity, but a decline in religious affiliation too.[4]

The decline in religiosity and/or religious affiliation does not mean that America is abandoning religion. It is still a very religious nation especially compared to other Western developed nations. The religiosity of some parts of the country has actually been compared to the religiosity of countries in the developing world. Gallup had this very intriguing title to an article on this which stated, "What Alabamians and Iranians Have in Common."[5] In 2007–2008, Gallup found that 82 percent of the population in Alabama agreed that religion was an important part of their daily life. That was nearly the same percentage in Iran (83%) on the same question in the same time period.

It should also be argued in this chapter that religion and religiosity is not a bad thing. That is not the interpretation that one should take away from this discussion. Religion helps people to deal with problems and think collectively and temporally. Since most religions conceive of an afterlife with stress upon living a good life as it pertains to others and their environment there is a cultivation of a social consciousness. This social consciousness extends beyond life itself especially for those religions that envision an afterlife full with bliss or perdition dependent on how one lived in this life and their legacy. The social consciousness aspect of religions has been associated with the reason religious people are generally happier than nonreligious people.[6] Religion encourages strong social ties with social support and the ability to release any guilt felt by the adherent. It helps to coordinate and orient people's behavior while cultivating trust and cooperation. A lack of any of these things generally makes people less happy.[7]

Religion has been associated with promoting a civil society and developing social capital.[8] A civil society is based on the self-organizing of people as they engage with each other and the larger community. In the United States this has traditionally developed around various community organizations like churches and other nongovernmental groups that simultaneously engage their members while influencing the society. This engagement has been considered a crucial ingredient in democracy in the United States as people develop ties between them that increase interdependency and trust.

The interdependence and trust along with the reassurances that most religions provide about the Hereafter increase psychological security. People desire both psychological as well as material security. An absence of this security particularly in countries where the government is either incapable or unwilling to provide it has been shown to increase religiosity among the population.[9]

As explained by the social psychologist Jonathan Haidt, people depend upon each other especially with others who see the world as they do for their emotional and material support.[10] This emphasizes the importance of group membership to religious identity and its connection to social support and happiness. This is described as sociocentricism and is considered an aspect of our evolution like our religious mindset. People formed groups to survive which generated modes of coexistence dependent on our underlying moral psychology which expresses itself in the religions we constructed to make sense of the world and give it meaning. As explained by Haidt, "there is now a great deal of evidence that religions do in fact help groups to cohere, solve free-rider problems and win the competition for group-level survival."[11]

These groups thrive on moral consistency which naturally reduces levels of internal diversity. It also creates problems with perceptions toward

Table 5.2 Correlation of Religiosity with the Number of Anti-Sharia Laws by State

	# of Anti-Sharia Laws
% Very Religious	.462*

Note: N = 50. *p ≤ .01 (two-tailed). Data from the Institute for Social Policy and Understanding (anti-Sharia laws) and Gallup (religiosity)

out-groups. Out-groups are viewed with suspicion or even hostility especially if in-group myths perpetuate beliefs about these out-groups that increase the level of threat perception. This concept is discussed in more detail in chapter 3 as it pertains to hate groups.

These dynamics become even more nefarious when people within these groups begin to direct anger toward these out-groups. Stanley Cohen referred to these people as moral entrepreneurs who invest in generating public anger toward marginalized people from these out-groups.[12] By pointing out how "starkly" different these groups are from the in-group and how they present a threat they aim to create a moral panic that will result in state action i.e. the use of state force by the dominant group or in the absence of a willing or capable government street-level violence and individual acts of prejudice.

This is where religion get its bad reputation. It's not necessarily the religion, but these group-based dynamics that lead to the simultaneous internal goods and external ills. The conundrum is that while religion is a beneficial thing for cultivating social cohesion, giving people meaning and generally increasing wellbeing it can lead to out-group oppression and conflict. It should also be noted that other things can stand in the place of religion with much less redeeming qualities like nationalism or racism. It is not like secularism has made our world a more peaceful place.

Religiosity is assumed to make these associations stronger. As one increases in commitment to one's faith there may be a greater inclination to strive for greater in-group consistency along with a greater out-group distaste. Again, this is not the case for all those that consider themselves very religious. A greater religiosity may indicate greater contentment with one's faith in which they find themselves at ease with those that are different from them. They do not become absorbed into group-based conflict and in many ways find hope and peace in the commonalities between people of different cultures and religions.

On the other hand, religiosity can do the opposite. As already discussed in chapter 2, Hewstone et al. found that religious salience, another term for religiosity, was associated with greater levels of Islamophobia.[13] When looking at the correlation between the introduction of anti-Sharia laws in the states from 2011 to 2017 (aggregate) and the average percentage of those that are very religious from 2012 to 2016, the correlation is significant and moderate. See table 5.2. This correlation shows that as the population in a state indicates that it is more religious, there is an association with the introduction of anti-Sharia laws.

The connection between religiosity and the introduction of anti-Sharia laws can be established by the increasing presence of religion in politics in the United States. As argued in chapter 4, among some branches of the Evangelical church and other denominations there has been an increasing political activism aimed at fulfilling their ideas of a perfect order based on their faith. The anti-Sharia movement is aimed at eliminating a threat to that order that is thoroughly grounded in those destructive group-based dynamics that can make religion disruptive in a multicultural society.

RELIGION AND POLITICS

In the United States today the line between religion and government is becoming increasingly distorted leading to new challenges. For example, many conservative movements have been attempting to spread policies that promote more religion in government through things such as faith-based initiatives. To this end, they have been mobilizing voters, engaging in lawsuits, spreading petitions and lobbying officials to increase the role of religion within the state. Naturally, this has led to increased tensions between religious proponents and their opponents as well as with religious believers of different faiths. This intrusion or some may argue the reassertion of religion in the state has not always been overt. For example, religious conservatives have been cultivating institutional activists within government to support their cause.[14]

Thomas Jefferson, one of the founders of the United States, argued for a "wall of separation" between the state and religion. This "wall," if it ever existed, has clearly crumbed over time and has mostly become vestigial.[15] Still, many founders like James Madison, who also advised against the overlap between religion and the state,[16] referred to the "Universal Sovereign" and one's duties to it. As explained by Haun, "duties to the 'Universal Sovereign' to use James Madison's term, are prior to—and take precedence over—duties to the political sovereign."[17] This language can be clearly linked to the language of the Puritans and any group that aims to assert religious dominance over the state.

Today, the activism of the Christian Right and its blending of religion and state has made the public uneasy with their activities and has fueled a "culture war" between liberals and conservatives. This is explored in more detail in chapter 7. Most Americans today do not support political activism by churches.[18] The fact that the Christian Right has been relatively unsuccessful politically is an example of this.[19] Still, those that support the political activism of churches show a willingness to accept religion in public policy.[20]

Still, religion and politics have historically interacted with each other in the United States. It has been argued that, "much of our political ferment historically and currently flows from religious commitments."[21] Alexis de Tocqueville found while touring the United States in the nineteenth Century that religion and politics were interconnected with each other.[22] Today, religion remains an important part of the political institutions in the country despite controversy surrounding its inclusion.[23] Keep in mind that the United States is still "one nation under God" with a currency that states "in God we trust." In the wake of tragedies it is common to offer "thoughts and prayers" and reference scripture during political speeches. Those same politicians are sworn into their office on some religious scripture.

Religion continues to play a role in political decision-making. Yamane and Oldmixon found that religion is a filter across different policy domains which inform policy goals.[24] Policies that focus upon education, the family, drugs, and foreign affairs are often informed by religious worldviews. Nicholas Martini found that religion influences policy choices, attitudes and beliefs.[25]

The connection between religion and public policy is likely unavoidable as argued by the late policy scholar, Hugh Heclo. Heclo argued that, "like it or not, modern government policy is invariably in the business of mandating, promoting, discouraging or prohibiting some ways of life and not others."[26] Opinions on those "ways of life" are likely derived from religion or religion-like thought. Some religious observants might consider prohibiting a way of life based on ideas and teachings found in scripture or the interpretations of that scripture.

According to Heclo, religion and policy interact for three reasons. First, the domains of religion and government overlap in substantive ways. Historically, religion has been concerned with education and social welfare which has become the prerogative of the government. Before the rise of modern governments, religious institutions provided these services. Even today, religious organizations still fulfill a vital role in education and public welfare. Increasingly, secular governments have encroached on this space creating tensions with these religious institutions.[27]

Second, the motivational factors of religion remain an important factor in society. As explained previously, religion has roots deep within human emotion. Religious motivation has generated some of the world's greatest feats. Those same religious motivations also encourage people to support certain policies. Politicians are aware of these motivations and will use religious language to describe a proposed bill to secure its passage. Those bills that are unambiguously based within religion generate even more religious zeal.[28]

Third, there are philosophical reasons for this overlap. Religion is argued to have a role within the state. There are teachings in many religions that have ramifications for the state as interpreted by some religious followers. These teachings are rules or values. The believers in these religions may advocate for the state to adopt these rules or values. For many, the dichotomy between the state and religion in secular society is defined by this separation in which religious rules and values are kept separate from the state. If these rules or values are adopted the interpretation is that religion played a tangential role in their adoption in order to make them appear more secular.[29]

Religiosity of the population matters the most for the level of interaction between the state and religion. Yamane and Oldmixon observed in their study that religiosity and how the religion is interpreted determines this interaction.[30] Freeman and Houston found while measuring religiosity by church attendance and prayer that religious commitment was a stronger predictor than religious affiliation for supporting clergy involvement in politics.[31] Goff and Trawick also found that denominational categories were not definitive for political positions.[32] Based on these studies, one may conclude that religious zeal is an important factor in determining political activism in support for policies based on religious ideas. One of these policies can certainly be the anti-Sharia laws.

Muslims are different religiously from Christians. Islam is a missionary faith like Christianity. Islam also does not recognize many core Christian beliefs such as the Trinity, Jesus being the Son of God and Jesus dying on the cross. In addition, Islam has increasingly been used to fill the unifying gap between the different conservative groups as the new external threat like communism was in the past. This has led to conservatives conflating Islam with other things of which they have an equal distaste. For example, Sam Nunberg, a former employee of the Trump campaign, referred to President Barack Obama as a socialist / Marxist and Islamo-fascist.[33] Somehow Islam got lumped in with fascism, socialism and Marxism, the three big scares of the American public.

NOTES

1. Jenkins, Jack. 2020. *American Prophets: The Religious Roots of Progressive Politics and the Ongoing Fight for the Soul of the Country*. New York: HarperCollins.
2. Ibid., 3.
3. Gallup. "Religion." Gallup.com. Last modified 2020. https://news.gallup.com/poll/1690/religion.aspx.
4. Cox, Daniel. "Millennials Are Leaving Religion And Not Coming Back." FiveThirtyEight. Last modified December 12, 2019. https://fivethirtyeight.com/features/millennials-are-leaving-religion-and-not-coming-back/.

5. Gallup. "What Alabamians and Iranians Have in Common." Gallup.com. Last modified February 9, 2009. https://news.gallup.com/poll/114211/alabamians-iranians-common.aspx.

6. "Are Religious People Happier, Healthier? Our New Global Study Explores This Question." Pew Research Center. Last modified May 30, 2020. https://www.pewresearch.org/fact-tank/2019/01/31/are-religious-people-happier-healthier-our-new-global-study-explores-this-question/.

7. Haidt, Jonathan. 2013. *The Righteous Mind: Why Good People are Divided by Politics and Religion.* New York: Vintage.

8. Houston, David J., Patricia K. Freeman, and David L. Feldman. 2008. "How Naked Is the Public Square? Religion, Public Service, and Implications for Public Administration." *Public Administration Review* 68, no. 3, 428–444.

9. Storm, Ingrid. 2017. "Does Economic Insecurity Predict Religiosity? Evidence from the European Social Survey 2002–2014." *Sociology of Religion* 78, no. 2, 146–172.

10. Hadit, *The Righteous Mind.*

11. Ibid, 298.

12. Cohen, Stanley. 2002. *Folk Devils and Moral Panics: The Creation of the Mods and Rockers.* London: Psychology Press.

13. Hewstone, Miles, Abigail Clare, Anna Newheiser, and Alberto Voci. 2011. "Making and unmaking prejudice: Religious affiliation reduces the impact of mortality salience on intergroup attitudes." *PsycEXTRA Dataset* 18, no. 3, 143–155.

14. Sager, Rebecca, and Keith Bentele. 2016. "Coopting the State: The Conservative Evangelical Movement and State-Level Institutionalization, Passage, and Diffusion of Faith-Based Initiatives." *Religions 7*, no. 6, 71.

15. Joppke, Christian. 2016. "Beyond the wall of separation: Religion and the American state in comparative perspective." *International Journal of Constitutional Law* 14, no. 4, 984–1008.

16. Merriman, Scott A. 2015. "What should the scales of justice balance? Historical aspects of the religious liberty debate." *Faulkner Law Review* 7, 79–103.

17. Haun, William J. 2020. "Religious Liberty and the Common Good." *National Affairs*, no. 44 (2020), 134.

18. Freeman & Houston, *US Public Opinion regarding Religious Involvement in Politics.*

19. Joppke, *Beyond the wall of separation.*

20. Freeman & Houston, *US Public Opinion regarding Religious Involvement in Politics.*

21. Elshtain, *Faith of Our Fathers and Mothers*, 39.

22. Elshtain, *Faith of Our Fathers and Mothers.*

23. Moots, *The Protestant Roots of American Civil Religion.*

24. Yamane, David, and Elizabeh A. Oldmixon. 2006. "Religion in the Legislative Arena: Affiliation, Salience, Advocacy, and Public Policymaking." *Legislative Studies Quarterly 31*, no. 3, 433–460.

25. Martini, Nicholas F. 2012. "'La Iglesia' in Politics? Religion and Latino Public Opinion." *Social Science Quarterly* 93, no. 4, 988–1006.

26. Heclo, Hugh. "Religion and Public Policy: An Introduction." *Journal of Policy History 13*, no. 1 (2001), 1–18.
27. Ibid.
28. Ibid.
29. Ibid.
30. Yamane and Oldmixon, *Religion in the Legislative Arena.*
31. Freeman and Houston, *US Public Opinion regarding Religious Involvement in Politics.*
32. Goff, Brian L., and Michelle W. Trawick. 2017. "Preaching and politics: disentangling religiosity and political choice." *Journal of Economics and Finance* 41, no. 3, 595–609.
33. Marantz, Andrew. 2019. *Antisocial: Online Extremists, Techno-Utopians, and the Hijacking of the American Conversation.* New York: Viking.

Chapter 6

Policy Diffusion

The analysis of the adoption of anti-Sharia laws by state governments in this book does not purport to be a policy diffusion study. The factors considered in this study are mostly environmental with a focus on demographic and political variables. Despite this, any analysis on this subject would be incomplete without considering the possibilities of policy diffusion. This is explored in this chapter.

The concept of policy diffusion was first conceptualized by Everett Rogers.[1] He is considered the "father of policy diffusion research."[2] The original idea was focused on the spread of ideas, but extended into public policy studies through the work of Frances Berry and William Berry.[3] The interest became how public policies spread across the United States. Some examples of this research include the adoption of education reforms,[4] abortion laws[5] and reforms to HMOs (Health Maintenance Organizations)[6] among other subjects. It has become a major public policy theory.

The argument in the theory is that a decision to adopt an idea, or in this case, a policy such as an anti-Sharia law involves several phases. First, there is an awareness of either the problem or the law as it was adopted in other jurisdictions. This is followed by knowledge and persuasion. It is during these stages that interactions with leaders from these other jurisdictions or with proponents of the law (anti-Muslim hate groups) will have their biggest effect. The lawmakers might have been aware of the "problem," but did not know how to address it or they did not even consider it a problem until these interactions. Considering that anti-Sharia laws are very political, political networks also would matter a lot for the spread of these laws.

Second, there is a decision by the lawmaker(s) to introduce the legislation. Once the law is introduced, the decision-making process may still involve those networks that led to the introduction of the law. The anti-Muslim groups would still be lobbying for it with individual legislators on various committees and in the chamber as a whole. Individual legislators would be consulting with others within their networks and considering how the law passed in other jurisdictions. This would include legal challenges to the bill, any political fallout and other outcomes from the law.

Third, if passed, the law will be implemented in the state where ideas from other jurisdictions will still matter as the courts would have to interpret it. Considering that the anti-Sharia laws are really targeted at the courts this would be the site for administrative decisions on the law. Assuming that the law is implemented in line with the intentions of the policymakers, this would then be confirmation particularly if the law is effective in achieving its desired ends. Although it is not clear what those ends are with anti-Sharia laws, one could assume that it's about keeping Sharia out of the courtroom in its various manifestations.

These decision phases assume a rational process for policy adoption based on interactions with other adopters (or proponents of adoption). The process assumes policy learning through observing others and either emulating them or competing with them. In some cases, such as when the Federal government imposes mandates on the states it's about coercion.[7]

Research in policy diffusion studies tries to answer questions related to policy adoption and the reasons for adoption. This includes why some places adopt earlier than others. In the case of the anti-Sharia laws, what is it about Tennessee and Oklahoma that made them the sites for the early adoption of this law? Further, this research also tries to understand the process for adoption. This may include an analysis of those decision networks and how those interactions translated into policy introduction and eventual adoption. The analysis in this book does not consider the process for adoption which is why this is not based within policy diffusion research. Still, there are many answers to the first question in this analysis as it is really focused on internal dynamics in these states such as religious composition, ideology and various political factors which are also important in diffusion studies.

SHARIA AND TERRORISM

One of the more interesting areas of the decision-making process outlined in the theory is in the learning phases. This is where it is assumed that anti-Muslim groups are most effective in getting these laws introduced in state legislatures. As already outlined in chapter 3, these groups have become integrated into larger networks which have strong ties to political parties and particular legislators. One could follow the campaign donations to ascertain the strength of those relationships, but anti-Sharia laws are mostly ideological which would require less incentive to introduce them and vote for them. At the core of the incentive for these laws is the establishment of some problem and making the case that this policy approach will address it. This is the traditional conceptualization of the policy process (stages model) which starts with the identification of a problem.

The problem with Sharia is usually defined as a problem with terrorism. Appeals to Western civilization and human rights are convincing if one is arguing that Sharia is what the Taliban was implementing in Afghanistan before 9/11. However, the culture in the United States was heavily influenced by John Stuart Mill, an English philosopher, who proposed in his principle of harm that the actions of people should only be limited if they harm others. If someone wants to follow a system of laws that limit their freedoms, then the state should not intervene unless that person is harming others. This is a core tenet of libertarianism, which has a strong following in the United States especially as the emphasis is on a limited government.

Instead, Sharia is linked with terrorism. The argument is that if one follows Sharia they are more likely to commit an act of terrorism. For those that equate Islam with terrorism, this is a given. This would be a violation of the harm principle and therefore necessitate the government to intervene to limit its practice. The challenge is in establishing the connection between Sharia and terrorism for the wider and less ideological public. The problem would have to be real and apparent. This would necessitate events, like 9/11, or what is referred to in policy studies as "policy windows" based on the work of John Kingdon.

In 2009, a year before the first anti-Sharia law was adopted, there were a number of high-profile terror attacks committed by Muslims. Umar Farouk Abdulmutallab attempted to down a plane with an explosive lined into his underwear. Abdulhakim Muhammad killed a soldier at an army recruiting station in Little Rock, Arkansas. The worst attack was by Major Nidal Malik Hasan who killed 13 soldiers at Ft. Hood in Texas. All of these individuals indicated that they were doing it because they were inspired by extremist rhetoric within networks of radical Muslims. Whether or not these events provided the policy window for the anti-Sharia laws is unknown, but they did provide ammunition for anti-Muslim groups to target the American Muslim community. For example, as discussed previously, Andy's Law is named after the soldier killed by Abdulhakim Muhammad in Little Rock.

Interestingly, terror attacks committed by Muslims in the United States declined to zero in 2011 and 2012 afterwards. The number of anti-Sharia bills introduced in state legislatures spiked in 2011. Refer back to figure 1.2

in chapter 1. After 2011, the number of bills introduced continued to decline with spikes in 2014, 2015, and 2017. Starting in 2013 the number of terror attacks perpetuated by Muslims started to increase along with the chaos in the Middle East following the Arab Spring and the civil war in Syria. See figure 6.1. The rise of the Islamic State of Iraq and Syria (ISIS) provided the perfect example of how Sharia and terrorism are cut from the same cloth.

In 2013 there was the Boston marathon attack by the Tsarnaev brothers. In 2015 Syed Rizwan Farook and his wife Tashfeen Malik attacked a county health building in San Bernardino, California. If these events were not enough, there was the Orlando nightclub shooting in 2016 by Omar Mateen. Yet, despite the spikes in bill introductions during this time period the general trend was downward. The critical moment remains 2009/2010, which not coincidently was the first year that President Barack Hussein Obama assumed office. A President that some assumed was a "closet Muslim," probably because of his name, and who made overtures to the Islamic world in his famous speech in Cairo in June 2009. Those who hated Muslims had much to be anxious about with President Obama. One might say that there was a perfect storm of electoral politics, terror attacks and the Manhattan mosque protest (referred to in chapters 1 and 2) that spurred on the anti-Sharia movement. All it took was a group of policy entrepreneurs, who might otherwise be known as the anti-Muslim hate groups covered in chapter 3.

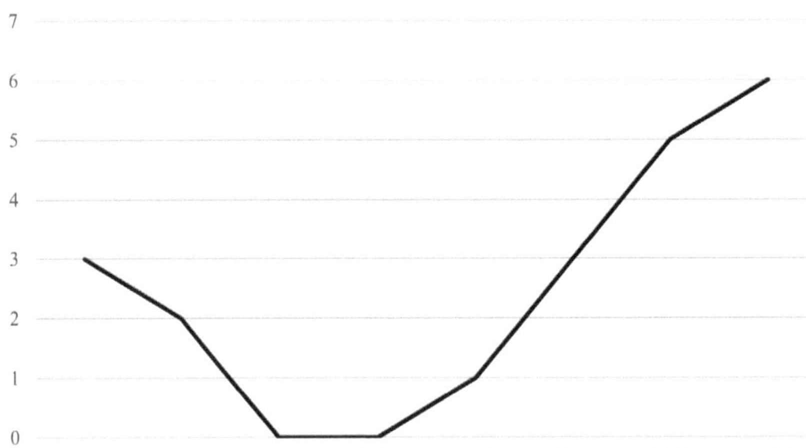

Figure 6.1 Number of Muslim-Extremist Terror Attacks in the United States (2009–2016). Data from the National Consortium for the Study of Terrorism and Responses to Terrorism at the University of Maryland.

DEFINING THE PROBLEM

In most policy theories, the definition of the problem is a really important starting point. Many of these problems are socially constructed even if there are focusing events that highlight the problem. If the connection between these events and the definition of the problem can be established, then policymakers focus their attention on addressing the problem.[8] Policy entrepreneurs would be critical in not only establishing this connection, but in proposing solutions to the problem. The proponents of the anti-Sharia laws would be working to make the case that there is a connection between Sharia and terrorism while also putting forward their solution to the problem. In fact, many of the anti-Sharia laws introduced into state legislatures followed the model legislation crafted by anti-Muslim hate groups almost to the letter.

Without assigning too much credit to the anti-Muslim hate groups, Islam already has a negative image. According to research at the Pew Research Center in Religion and Public Life, Muslims are the least popular religious group in the United States coming in slightly below Atheists. This popularity declines with older groups and Republicans.[9] Given this negative image it is not particularly difficult to link Sharia with terrorism.

Policies diffuse when the policy design is seen as appropriate in addressing the problem or the target population. Those populations (groups) that have a stigmatized social image often receive the burdens of public policy. These groups are seen as deviants which merit the adversarial policy. These policies are often enacted into law. The fate of these policies is often determined by the strength of the affected group. The stronger the group (politically) the less likely these burdens will be enacted into law.[10]

Muslims in the United States have a stigmatized identity.[11] They face various forms of discrimination on a daily basis. This is more so for those that are "apparently Muslim" that is, because of their names, ethnic background or clothing they wear. As already established in chapter 2, Islamophobia is a problem in the United States as elsewhere. Much of this is based within a general narrative around Islam and Muslims that promotes an image that they are threatening outsiders. This narrative can be seen in movies[12] and in the media.[13]

According to the Narrative Policy Framework, another popular public policy theory, groups use policy narratives to influence public policy. At the individual level, these narratives are used to influence people who will support certain policy solutions assuming the group and their policy entrepreneurs draw those connections. All one needs is a focusing event and one has policy change.[14] The confluence of a general narrative around Islam coupled with anti-Muslim hate groups that are using that narrative along with useful focusing events to connect a supposed problem with a recommended solution aids in the spread of these policies.

FACTORS FOR POLICY DIFFUSION

According to research on policy diffusion, there are a number of factors that are commonly identified in the literature for the spread of policies between jurisdictions. There are internal dynamics like the demographics of the place, which is the focus of the analysis in this book. The kind of policy also matters. Highly technical and less salient policies tend to spread slower because of the lack of public knowledge or interest in the policy. The less complex and more salient a policy, the faster it spreads because the public is better able to understand it and see it as an important area. The relative costs of a policy are an important factor especially for the policymakers in charge of the budget. When a policy is mostly symbolic with little attached to it in regards to expense, this policy tends to spread faster. It allows the policymaker to score points without having to make difficult budgetary decisions.[15]

There are many reasons to believe that anti-Sharia laws are less complex and more salient policies prone to spread fast among certain states. They are not overly technical. Their intention is pretty clear with their effects mostly limited to the courts. The group being targeted is also clear especially since the early versions of the law explicitly states Sharia. The later versions of the law only mentioned "foreign law," but when this version was introduced by the same legislator who introduced the former, more explicit law it is clear what is meant by "foreign law." Besides changing how courts hear cases and which legal perspective to consider, there are not substantive changes that require great expense from these laws. According to policy diffusion theory, there is little to stop the spread of these laws except internal dynamics and legal challenges.

One recurring factor included in policy diffusion studies is geographical proximity. According to the theory, there is reason to believe that when jurisdictions border each other they strive to imitate each other. Some of this is due to similar populations with similar internal dynamics. There is also interjurisdictional competition. When a policy has been proposed in a competing jurisdiction, there is pressure for that jurisdiction to adopt a similar policy. This is especially the case if the policy is popular among their constituents.

Anti-Sharia laws are already prone for diffusion as established in this chapter. There is a general narrative plus the activism of hate groups that make them popular among certain groups of people. When adopted by one neighboring state, the pressure for adoption increases especially if the demographics of that state are similar to the adopting state. When looking at the map for policy adoption (see figure 1.1), one can see a concentration of states in the South that have adopted the law.

One way to measure geographical proximity in policy diffusion studies is through a percentage of neighboring jurisdictions with a contiguous border that have adopted the law. In one of the few studies on state adoption of anti-Sharia laws, Mitchell and Toner studied the diffusion of these laws. The authors included this variable which they found to be one of the significant reasons for diffusion.[16] This variable has been included in the analysis in this book.

NOTES

1. Rogers, Everett M. 1962. *Diffusion of Innovations*. New York: Simon and Schuster.
2. Mcgrath, Cathleen, and Deone Zell. 2001. "The Future of Innovation Diffusion Research and its Implications for Management." *Journal of Management Inquiry* 10, no. 4, 386–391.
3. Berry, Frances S., and William D. Berry. 1990. "State Lottery Adoptions as Policy Innovations: An Event History Analysis." *American Political Science Review* 84, no. 2, 395–415.
4. Mintrom, Michael. 1997. "The State-Local Nexus in Policy Innovation Diffusion: The Case of School Choice." *Publius: The Journal of Federalism* 27, no. 3, 41–60.
5. Mooney, Christopher Z., and Mei-Hsien Lee. 1995. "Legislative Morality in the American States: The Case of Pre-Roe Abortion Regulation Reform." *American Journal of Political Science* 39, no. 3, 599–627.
6. Balla, Steven J. 2001. "Interstate Professional Associations and the Diffusion of Policy Innovations." *American Politics Research* 29, no. 3, 221–245.
7. Gilardi, Fabrizio. 2016. "Four Ways We Can Improve Policy Diffusion Research." *State Politics & Policy Quarterly* 16, no. 1, 8–21.
8. Boushey, Graeme. 2010. *Policy Diffusion Dynamics in America*. Cambridge: Cambridge University Press.
9. Mitchell, Travis. "How Americans Feel About Different Religious Groups." Pew Research Center's Religion & Public Life Project. Last modified May 30, 2020. https://www.pewforum.org/2017/02/15/americans-express-increasingly-warm-feelings-toward-religious-groups/.
10. Boushey, Graeme. 2016. "Targeted for Diffusion? How the Use and Acceptance of Stereotypes Shape the Diffusion of Criminal Justice Policy Innovations in the American States." American Political Science Review 110, no. 1, 198–214.
11. Hummel, Daniel, Mohamed Daassa, Nuha Alshabani, and Leen Felo. 2020. "Identifying as Muslim and American: The Role of Discrimination." Review of Religious Research 62, no. 3, 465–483.
12. Shaheen, Jack G. 2003. *Reel Bad Arabs: How Hollywood Vilifies a People*, 3rd ed. Northampton, MA: Olive Branch Pr.

13. Kearns, Erin M., Allison E. Betus, and Anthony F. Lemieux. 2019. "Why Do Some Terrorist Attacks Receive More Media Attention Than Others?" *Justice Quarterly* 36, no. 6, 985-1022.

14. Jones, M., E. Shanahan, and M. McBeth. 2014. *The Science of Stories: Applications of the Narrative Policy Framework in Public Policy Analysis.* Basingstoke: Springer.

15. Douglas, James W., Ringa Raudla, and Roger E. Hartley. 2015. "Shifting Constellations of Actors and Their Influence on Policy Diffusion: A Study of the Diffusion of Drug Courts." *Policy Studies Journal* 43, no. 4, 484–511.

16. Mitchell, Joshua L., and Brendan Toner. 2016. "Exploring the Foundations of US State-Level Anti-Sharia Initiatives." *Politics and Religion* 9, no. 4, 720–743.

Chapter 7

Political Culture War

The political culture war is a reference to political divisions between the political Right (conservatives) and Left (progressives) in the United States. Evidence of this division can be found not only in party platforms, but in voting patterns on legislation. According to the Pew Research Center, the polarization in Congress has roots in the 1970s based on ideological scores for senators and representatives. In the 1970s there was still considerable overlap between members of Congress from different parties. By 2011/12 there was no overlap at all.[1] This stark contrast was shown in an animation produced by Business Insider which shows connections between House members with their votes. The animation shows the 1990s as the period for increasing polarization which became even more stark in the 2000s and 2010s.[2]

The political culture war includes many issues both moral and economic. Economically, this has included divisions over healthcare and the insurance industry. The Affordable Care Act signed into law by President Barack Obama in 2010 created much controversy for those on the political Right who saw it as a step toward "socialized medicine." The law called for an expansion of the Medicaid program and imposed a penalty for not having health insurance for those that did not qualify for this program. The TEA (Taxed Enough Already) Party formed around opposition to this law because they saw it as an expansion of the scope of government that would increase costs which would ultimately lead to an increase in taxes. There were other divisive economic issues that increased the divide such as the minimum wage and right-to-work laws.

Moral issues are usually focused on marriage and reproductive rights. Those on the political Right oppose any conception of marriage that is not between a man and a woman. Some states had this built into their constitutions and they rallied around the Defense of Marriage Act passed in the 1990s and repeatedly challenged in court. Sections of the law have been superseded by court decisions with the most consequential of them being *Obergefell* v. *Hodges* (2015) which mandated that states recognize same-sex marriage as a civil right.

Abortion continues to be a controversial moral issue with those on the political Right equating it with legalized murder and those on the political Left arguing for an increase in control women have over their own bodies. Some states have stopped short of forbidding the practice since it was legalized by the Supreme Court in *Roe* v. *Wade* (1973). They have increasingly made it more difficult to get one along with private companies refusing to include abortion services among coverages in their health insurance.

In between economic and moral issues that characterize the culture war is nationalism defined through religion, race or both. The anti-immigrant/anti-refugee movement resides here with those on the political Right arguing that those who are White or of the Judeo-Christian faith are slowly being replaced by non-White immigrants or Muslims. An anti-immigrant attitude is not necessarily based entirely within a nationalistic mindset as there are economic concerns if it is true that immigrants are taking the jobs of born-and-raised Americans. This is not true. There are also moral concerns if refugees are jeopardizing public safety and increasing crime in the community. Again, this is not true. Often times, nationalistic arguments are framed this way though.

These three areas (morality, economics, and nationalism) define the political culture war in the United States. They are not mutually exclusive areas with considerable overlap between them especially within electoral politics. It is possible to see Islam and the Muslim American community as an affront to those with a nationalistic perspective as well as those with a moralist perspective. This is especially if Islam is framed as a threat with morals, defined by Sharia, that are an antithesis to the West. Those with this perspective see the necessity of an anti-Sharia law to contain this threat.

The stark differences between those on the political Right and Left leave little room for common ground between the two groups. Many of these issues are highly ideological. Islam presents a particular challenge to this as many salient issues to the moralists on the political Right are relevant to the Muslim community, another faith group, but Islamophobia prevents Muslims from joining these movements. On the other side, those on the political Left view the Muslim community as a marginalized group under attack by conservatives, yet the religious beliefs and practices of Muslims are not welcome. If common ground can be rediscovered between political orientations as well as religious groups much of this would be a moot point.

COMMON GROUND AND MYTHOS-THINKING

There is much moral diversity between groups in the United States. Moral diversity is the celebration of different values by different groups. Moral diversity can cause conflicts over values that make a utilitarian approach appealing for decision-makers. John Rawls argued that procedural values like fairness and ethics are needed in this type of environment.[3] The expectation was that identity would not matter as procedural values would apply to all equally. Logos-thinking dominates from this perspective and is considered the approach of the United States when it passes and implements its laws. This is also why some have labeled the United States a logocracy.[4]

People are mythos-thinkers and need common values to bind them. Fairness alone is not satisfying. Haidt explained that those on the political Left refer frequently to the value of fairness without mentioning or appreciating other values that have to do with sacredness. According to Haidt, this is not satisfying to people in society and is one of the reasons those on the political Right continue to be successful at the ballot box in the United States.[5] The impetus on forming bonds with those of similar values might explain why Putnam found negative effects from diversity on the formation of social capital that is, trust.[6,7]

Each individual has a narrative about themselves and how they fit in with the larger society. There is also a historical narrative which is about the larger society and the institutions that represent it. The unity that develops between people in that society is based within the level of overlap between the individual narrative and the historical narrative. The argument goes, the greater the overlap the more unity between people. This overlap is the common ground.[8]

Common ground is required to overcome the challenges of diversity to societal cohesiveness. Public deliberation can help to form a consensus between different value groups.[9] In many ways, it's about understanding each other's narratives and their larger connections. Logos-thinking is not the only source for this common ground especially since mythos-thinking is so important to people and society. Logos-thinking is seemingly safer, but has been unsatisfying leading to criticism of this approach by important scholars like Dwight Waldo and David Hume. They appreciated that human rationality was dependent on emotion and that this was unlikely to change. Emotion and sacredness are directly connected with each other. In the United States, individual and historical narratives are often based within religious experiences.[10]

Although diversity presents challenges to finding common narratives, Mark Cladis argued that there are shared narratives, aspirations, and common projects between diverse groups.[11] In this regard, there should be plenty of opportunities for diverse groups to find common ground. Unfortunately, this is not the case today. The lack of the ability to find common ground through a mythos-framework in an increasingly diverse environment with divergent ideas on sacredness has increased conflict in the United States. This void has been filled with various fundamentalist ideologies some religious and some not religious.

It is common to associate these divisions with the political Right and conservatives. They certainly have a hand in this, but those on the political Left have also engaged in a certain kind of absolutism toward their own values. Elshtain explained the existence of liberal monism. Liberal monism stresses a single standard of what counts as reason and deliberation. This standard is enforced in a religious manner much like a constraint on thought and action often associated with religion.[12] Uddin called this secular repressive which is an imposition of secular values upon everyone including religious people.[13] Rothman felt that this way of thinking was more evident among the more progressive branches in liberal thought such as with the social justice movement that has increasingly become more identitarian i.e. combining identity politics with social justice activism. Rothman added, "when this identity politics is fused with the obligations that social justice activists see as vital collective imperatives, you get something that resembles a religion."[14]

It should be pointed out that religion or things that resemble religion do not have to be absolute or divisive. The religious Left is an example of multi-faith activism in which different religious groups work together on what they have in common. Typically, they are working toward social justice from an intersectional perspective. They understand that prejudice is rarely limited to a single group and their advocacy for equal treatment spans racial, religious, ethnic, and sexual identity groups.[15] As explained previously, progressives have had an uncomfortable coexistence with the religious Left despite having common interests.

On the other side of the political spectrum, their activism is rarely inclusive of the same groups on the political Left. The presidential campaign of then-candidate Donald Trump was the culmination of politicized conservative Christianity over the decades. Even though 80 percent of White Evangelicals supported him, his candidacy deeply divided the Evangelical base in the Republican Party. This highlighted that far from being an expression of religious fervor, Trump's candidacy bolstered what is known as Christian nationalism. Jenkins explained, "Christian nationalism isn't a religious term defined by nuanced theological structures; it isn't even tied exclusively to white evangelicalism. Instead, it functions primarily as an identity that largely exists outside of a specific religious moral code."[16] Thus that movement has more to do with nationalism than any traditional moral or economic concerns that typify the Republican Party. Despite this, Trump and his supporters worked to ensure overlap between his true platform, populist nationalism, and the traditional platforms of those focused on moral or economic issues. This overlap was almost entirely based within political narratives that capitalized on the political culture war. Islam and the Muslim community became a convenient target that solidified divergent interests. One might argue it was a conservative unity through political division.

CONSERVATIVES AND ISLAM

According to Smith, conservatism in the United States has three sources in the modern era. The first source is Lockean laissez-faire based off the ideas of John Locke. This emphasizes the market and free choice over the intervention of the government. The second source is tradition which is the domain of the religious conservatives. This is the branch of conservatism that emphasizes external structures and constraints that is in conflict with free choice conservatives. The third source is the hostility to Communism especially during the Cold War. The hostility to Communism bound these three groups together.[17]

This categorization by Smith is similar to the categorization outlined in this book. The laissez-faire perspective is focused on economic issues. A free market is preferable to government regulation which also includes taxes. Taxes are seen as a distortion to the free market. An increase in government programs, particularly entitlement spending, increases the propensity for the government to increase taxes. This was the anxiety around the Affordable Care Act.

The traditional perspective with religious conservatives is focused on moral issues. As discussed previously, these moral issues tend to be focused on abortion and marriage, but have included other areas. This form of conservatism is concerned with the "Good Society" as defined by moral values. These values originate within religious texts and church doctrine.

The hostility to Communism is embedded in nationalism in the United States. The Cold War increased nationalistic feelings especially with those on the political Right. There were concerns about communist infiltration which gave rise to paranoid reactions like McCarthyism. It is not difficult to see these same paranoid reactions with Muslims and Sharia.

Muqtedar Khan outlined five different perspectives on Islam in the United States. Two of these are liberal perspectives where Islam is not seen as a threat. The other three perspectives are conservative perspectives with very different views toward Islam. The first perspective is the "traditional conservative" perspective. The views of Bernard Lewis and Samuel Huntington are represented here. Islam is seen as the problem. Khan explained, "Lewis' indictment of Islam includes a dogmatic assertion that Islam is incompatible with democracy, liberalism, secularism and modernity, and since America is the epitome of these values, Muslims are anti-American."[18] Huntington also claimed that Islam is incompatible with democracy.[19] These conservatives are more likely to question the patriotism of American Muslims. This version of conservatism informs the Trump administration's view of the American Muslim community. Lajevardi and Abrajano found that resentment toward Muslim Americans was a strong and significant predictor of support for Trump.[20] These conservatives are more closely aligned with the nationalists.

Khan described two other conservative perspectives on Islam. The "neo-conservative" perspective differentiates militant Islam from the rest of the Islamic community. They believe in the narrative of the "good Muslim" versus the "bad Muslim." They reject the idea that Islam is a threat to the West or that Islam is not compatible with democracy.[21] These conservatives are more in line with the laissez-faire conservatives who are more focused on the economy and less on issues of morality or nationalism. This version of conservatism informed the George W. Bush's administration view of the American Muslim community.

The other perspective outlined by Khan is the "realist" perspective. This perspective takes an empirical view of Islam in which terrorism is an outgrowth of politics or economics.[22] Islam is not necessarily the problem, but it is interpreted in a problematic way when the political or economic situation disadvantages Muslims. Violent Islamic movements are shaped by their violent environments.[23] The late Alan Krueger found that despite most terrorists being better educated and well-off, they were motivated by the social problems around them.[24] The lack of justice in cases involving Muslims, discriminatory policies, and poverty and political repression in Muslim-majority countries can all be lightning rods for extremism. Countries that suppress political/civil rights and liberties breed extremist perspectives.[25] Shadi Hamid also made this case in his book on Islamic exceptionalism. He argued, "the gap between what Muslims once were and where they now find themselves is at the center of the anger and humiliation driving political violence across the Middle East."[26]

This perspective informs much of the academic discourse around Islam and terrorism. Bureaucrats and career politicians have also largely embraced this perspective, but within the conservative movement in the United States today the traditional perspective is growing in popularity. According to a report by Muslim Advocates, in 2018 80 anti-Muslim candidates ran for political office.[27] Although only 14 percent of them were actually elected, the frequency of the use of anti-Muslim tropes to get elected has been increasing over time. For example, the label "Muslim" was used as a slur against President Obama which even liberals worked to disprove. In fact, the only people to stand up and say, "so what if he is Muslim" were "realist" conservatives like Colin Powell.[28]

FACTORS FOR ANTI-SHARIA LAWS

Given the close association between conservatism and Islamophobia, an assumption is that as the population of a state increases in conservatism the more likely that state is to have an anti-Sharia law. This association may be stronger when another state with a similar ideology adopts the law. One measure that captures this is ideological distance. This is calculated by adding the average of the percentage conservative of the most recent adopters of the law (one year ago) with the average of the percentage conservative from two years ago and creating an average of these two percentages. From this value, subtract the percentage conservative in a state at the time of adoption. It is assumed that as the ideological distance increases between adopting states the less likely the state will adopt the law. Gallup collects annual surveys from residents in these states asking if their political views are very conservative, conservative, moderate, liberal, or very liberal. The percentage of those with political views that are very conservative and conservative can be compared with the percentage of those with political views that are very liberal and liberal to construct ideological distance measures.[29] This measure has been included in the analysis in this book.

Another measure on political dominance in a state can possibly capture the effects of the political culture war on the introduction and adoption of an anti-Sharia law. Since most Republicans identify as conservative and most Democrats identify as liberal, an assumption is that as Democratic dominance in a state increases that state is less likely to have an anti-Sharia law. Austin Ranney developed the Ranney index to determine the level of political competition in a state ranging from 1 (Democratic control) to 0 (Republican control).[30] This measure can also be used to determine if political consolidation (Democratic or Republican) is important for law introduction and adoption. Ideologically-driven policies like the anti-Sharia laws may be unpopular in states that are evenly split between political parties because of the influence of moderates. This measure is part of the analysis in this book.

The influence of moderates in swing states may also have something to do with the level of professionalism of the legislature. States with full time legislatures are considered more professional than part time legislatures. Another assumption is that more professional legislatures are less likely to introduce or pass an anti-Sharia law. This may be due to a focus on more substantive legislation and less on symbolic legislation. Anti-Sharia laws do more harm than good and a more professional legislature would avoid this type of frivolous legislation. Peverill Squire developed the Squire index to capture the level of professionalism of state legislatures.[31] The more professional a legislature higher the score on the Squire Index. This measure has been incorporated into the analysis in this book.

Professionalism in a legislature also alludes to the possible effects of education in the general population. It is assumed that a more educated population would be less likely to support the adoption of an anti-Sharia law as it would mostly be seen as addressing pseudo-problems. This population would have gone to college with a diverse student body including Muslims and might have had classes on Islam that would have got into the nuances of the faith and how it is practiced around the world. The inter-group contact hypothesis supports the idea that increased contact decreases discriminatory attitudes toward out-groups.[32] The proportion with a Bachelor's degree or higher is a measure of educational achievement in a state. This measure has been adopted in the analysis in this book.

NOTES

1. DeSilver, Drew. "The Polarized Congress of Today Has Its Roots in the 1970s." Pew Research Center. Last modified May 30, 2020. https://www.pewresearch.org/fact-tank/2014/06/12/polarized-politics-in-congress-began-in-the-1970s-and-has-been-getting-worse-ever-since/.

2. "This 60-second Animation Shows How Divided Congress Has Become Since 1949." Business Insider. Last modified September 11, 2019. https://www.businessinsider.com/animation-rise-partisanship-congress-house-representatives-60-years-2016-4.

3. Rothman, Noah. 2019. *Unjust: Social Justice and the Unmaking of America*. New York: Simon & Schuster.

4. Olehla, Richard. 2010. "Common Faith: Civil Religion in the US." *New Presence: The Prague Journal of Central European Affairs* 14, no. 2, 26–31.

5. Haidt, Jonathan. 2013. *The Righteous Mind: Why Good People are Divided by Politics and Religion*. New York: Vintage, 239.

6. Putnam, Robert D. 2001 *Bowling Alone*. New York: Simon & Schuster.

7. Hewstone, Miles. 2015. "Consequences of Diversity for Social Cohesion and Prejudice: The Missing Dimension of Intergroup Contact." *Journal of Social Issues 71*, no. 2, 417–438.

8. Braunstein, Ruth. 2018. "A (More) Perfect Union? Religion, Politics, and Competing Stories of America." *Sociology of Religion* 79, no. 2, 172–195.

9. Casanova, Jose. 2001. "Religion, the New Millennium, and Globalization." *Sociology of Religion 62*, no. 4, 415.

10. Braunstein, *A (More) Perfect Union?*

11. Cladis, Mark S. 2008. "Painting Landscapes of Religion in America: Four Models of Religion in Democracy." *Journal of the American Academy of Religion* 76, no. 4, 874–904.

12. Elshtain, Jean B. 2001. "Faith of Our Fathers and Mothers: Religious Belief and American Democracy." In *Religion in American Public Life: Living with Our Deepest Differences*, edited by Jean B. Elshtain and Azizah Y. Hibri. New York: W. W. Norton & Company, 39–61.

13. Uddin, Asma T. 2019. *When Islam Is Not a Religion: Inside America's Fight for Religious Freedom*. Farmington Hills, MI: Pegasus Books.

14. Rothman, *Unjust*, 5.

15. Jenkins, Jack. 2020. *American Prophets: The Religious Roots of Progressive Politics and the Ongoing Fight for the Soul of the Country*. New York: HarperCollins.

16. Ibid, 61.

17. Smith, Robert C. 2010. *Conservatism and Racism, and Why in America They Are the Same*. Albany: SUNY Press.

18. Khan, Muqtedar. 2018. *Five American Perspectives on Islam: An Analytical Perspective*. Washington, DC: Center for Global Policy. https://www.cgpolicy.org/wp-content/uploads/2018/02/Special_Report.pdf.

19. Huntington, Samuel P. 1984. "Will More Countries Become Democratic?" *Political Science Quarterly 99*, no. 2, 193.

20. Lajevardi, Nazita, and Marisa Abrajano. 2019. "How Negative Sentiment toward Muslim Americans Predicts Support for Trump in the 2016 Presidential Election." *The Journal of Politics* 81, no. 1, 296–302.

21. Khan, *Five American Perspectives on Islam*.

22. Ibid.

23. Meral, Ziya. 2018. *How Violence Shapes Religion: Belief and Conflict in the Middle East and Africa*. Cambridge: Cambridge University Press.

24. Krueger, Alan B. 2008. *What Makes a Terrorist: Economics and the Roots of Terrorism*. Princeton: Princeton University Press.

25. Uddin, *When Islam Is Not a Religion*.

26. Hamid, Shadi. 2016. *Islamic Exceptionalism: How the Struggle Over Islam Is Reshaping the World*. New York: St. Martin's Press.

27. Muslim Advocates. *Running on Hate Update: Anti-Muslim Candidates Underperform in Last Night's Elections*. Washington, DC, July 1, 2018. https://muslimadvocates.org/2018/11/running-on-hate-update-anti-muslim-candidates-underperform-in-last-nights-elections/.

28. Hasan, Mehdi. "Colin Powell on Obama's "Muslim" Faith." Global Current Affairs, Politics & Culture. Last modified August 20, 2010. https://www.newstatesman.com/blogs/mehdi-hasan/2010/08/obama-muslim-iraq-powell.

29. Grossback, Lawrence J., Sean Nicholson-Crotty, and David A. Peterson. 2004. "Ideology and Learning in Policy Diffusion." *American Politics Research 32*, no. 5, 521–545.

30. Klarner, Carl. "Other Scholars? Competitiveness Measures." Harvard Dataverse. Last modified September 10, 2013. https://dataverse.harvard.edu/dataset.xhtml?persistentId=doi:10.7910/DVN/QSDYLH.

31. Squire, Peverill. 2017. "A Squire Index Update." *State Politics & Policy Quarterly 17*, no. 4, 361–371.

32. Schmid, Katharina, Ananthi A. Ramiah, and Miles Hewstone. 2014. "Neighborhood Ethnic Diversity and Trust." *Psychological Science 25*, no. 3, 665–674.

Chapter 8

Analysis and Results

The previous chapters outlined those factors mostly likely to influence whether a state has an anti-Sharia law. These factors are summarized here. The first factor (chapter 6) is the percentage of neighboring states that have adopted the bill between 2010 and 2019. This timeframe is based on when the law was first adopted in 2010 and the last year of available data for this study. It is assumed that a state with a greater percentage of neighboring states with an anti-Sharia law also adopts the law.

The second factor (chapter 7) is the ideological distance variable. This compares the ideology of adopting states from previous years to current adopting states. The focus is on conservatism since it has been established in this book that there is an association between conservatism and Islamophobia in the United States. It is assumed that as the conservative population in a state increases it is more likely there will be an anti-Sharia law in that state. Further, it is assumed that when a state has a similar level of the conservative population as an adopting state it is more likely that state will also have an anti-Sharia law. Data on the size of the conservative population are from Gallup surveys.

The third factor (chapter 3) is the presence of anti-Muslim groups in a state. This measure is based on the percentage of all hate groups in 2017. This is the last year of data available at the time of this study. The proportion of these hate groups out of all hate groups shows the level of the presence and activity of anti-Muslim groups in a state. These groups lobby for anti-Sharia laws and use anti-Muslim narratives that disparage Muslims to secure support for them among legislators and the public. Data on hate groups are available from the Southern Poverty Law Center. It is assumed that as this percentage increases it is more likely that a state will have an anti-Sharia law.

The fourth factor (chapter 4) is the size of the Evangelical Christian community in a state. It has been established in this book that among some Evangelicals there is apparent Islamophobia. Based on this association, it is assumed that as this population increases in a state it is more likely that there is an anti-Sharia law. This measure is based on data from the Association of Religion Data Archives in 2010 (the last religious census) and is a percentage of the state population.

The fifth factor (chapter 5) is religious salience or religiosity. It is assumed that as religiosity increases there is an increased chance that the state has an anti-Sharia law. As discussed in this book there is an association between religiosity and Islamophobia. Those states with a larger percentage of their population that are very religious are more likely to have an anti-Sharia law based on this assumption. Data on religiosity by state is available from Gallup for the years 2012–2016.

The sixth factor (chapter 7) is political competition or a measure of Democratic control of a state. It is assumed that as a state is more democratically controlled it is less likely that a state will have an anti-Sharia law. This assumption is based within the political culture war explored in chapter 7. Further, it may also reveal that states that have more political competition, that is, with measures in the middle of the scale are less likely to adopt these laws because of competition over independents who are less ideologically driven. This measure is based on the Ranney Index calculated on a four-year moving average between 2007 and 2010.[1] This was the last time the Index was calculated and provides a good snapshot of political competitiveness for each state leading into the first year of anti-Sharia law adoption.

The seventh factor (chapter 7) is the level of legislative professionalism. As discussed in chapter 7, the Squire measure is used to capture this professionalism. It is assumed that as the professionalism increases in a legislature it is less likely that a state will adopt this law. This measure was last calculated in 2015.[2]

The eighth factor (chapter 7) is education. This is calculated as the percentage with a Bachelor's degree or higher of the total population. The data from 2010 for this variable is used in this study since there is little year-to-year variability and provides a good starting point for understanding the passage of these laws by the first few states. These data are from the US Census. It is assumed that a more educated population would be less likely to support the adoption of an anti-Sharia law as it would mostly be seen as addressing pseudo-problems.

These eight factors are the focus of this study. Although these factors are not an exhaustive list of possible explanations for policy adoption, they have been used in previous studies on this topic.[3] There are two outcome variables of interest. The most interesting outcome is whether a state has an anti-Sharia law. The years for this outcome encompass the study period (2010 to 2019). This is a simple dichotomous variable in which a state either has the law or not. The other outcome variable is the number of times that law was introduced in a state. This is a count variable as the law has been introduced a number of times in some states. Both variables measure interest in the law, but there are differences between states that adopt the law and those that simply introduce it. Given the challenges of policymaking, it takes incredible momentum for a bill to become a law. Introducing the law show enthusiasm for the law for some legislators, but passing the law may say more about these factors in this study. The goal of this analysis is to understand the possible relationships between these factors and the introduction / passage of anti-Sharia laws.

The descriptive statistics for these variables are in table 8.1. Between 2010 and 2019, in one state the bill was introduced more than 20 times while in other states it was never introduced at all. 12 states have passed the law since 2010. Some of these states have more than half of their population that is Evangelical Christian while the average population of Muslims is less than 1 percent. On average, religiosity is close to 40 percent with some states above 60 percent. The standard deviation values for each of the variables indicate variability between the states.

The interest in this study is whether these variables are related to either bill introduction or bill passage. This is not an analysis of the process for passage of these bills so the motivations for passage can only be inferred from this analysis. It is assumed that political, economic, religious, geographic, and demographic factors have an effect on introducing and/or passing the

Table 8.1 Descriptive Statistics of Variables

	Mean	*Max. Value*	*Min. Value*	*Std. Dev.*
Bill Introduced	4.42	22	0	4.9
Years to Passage	8.6	10	1	2.7
% Evangelical	13.2	55	1.2	12.05
% Muslim	0.47	2.8	0.03	0.65
Ideological Distance	4.9	19.5	-6.5	5.98
% Neighbor Adopt	18.2	83	0	25.7
Ranney Index	0.53	1	0	0.32
Squire Index	0.225	0.629	0.048	0.105
Religiosity	39.9	60.25	21	9
% Higher Education	27.16	38.3	17.3	4.8

Note: Bill introduction and passage data from the Southern Poverty Law Center. % Evangelical and Muslim data from the Association of Religion Data Archives. Ideological distance calculated using % Conservative data from Gallup and the method of Grossback et al. (2004). % Neighbor Adopt data are based on the percentage of contiguous states that have adopted the law at the time of adoption. The Ranney Index data are from a four-year average between 2007 and 2010 (Klarner, 2013). Squire Index data are from Squire (2017). Religiosity data are from Gallup (2012 - 2016). % Higher Education data are from the U.S. Census.

law. This is the research question in this study that is, what are the effects of political, economic, religious, geographic, and demographic factors on bill introduction and adoption? The word adoption is used loosely here to simply indicate that the bill was passed without explaining the political rationale of those that passed it. The example of the Florida law in the Introduction shows that for most the interest in the law is ideological which these factors can help explain, but for some it is based on other political calculations. There is always a risk in these types of analyses to reduce the dynamics behind these bills, but generalization is a useful first step in understanding these dynamics. The next section explains the design of this study.

STUDY DESIGN

A standard approach to assessing the factors for whether a state has a policy or not is an event history analysis. This is typically executed through a Cox regression. As noted by Allison, "Cox regression is unequivocally the best all-around method for estimating regression models for event history data."[4] This technique assesses the relationship between the survival time and the covariates in the model. The outcome is the log of the hazard ratio at time (t). A significant relationship between a covariate and the outcome is determined at the .05 probability level. Interpretation of the effect is based on the odds ratio.

Another common approach is to use a logistic regression. The outcome variable would be whether a state has a policy or not. The goal of this approach is to predict the probability of the outcome (a state has an anti-Sharia law) as compared to a state not having the law. The acceptable significance level is the same and the interpretation is also based on the odds ratio. Both approaches are included in this study to compare results.

The other method adopted in this study is a Poisson regression. The outcome in the Cox and logistic regressions is focused on policy adoption. The outcome in the Poisson regression is focused on bill introduction i.e. the number of times an anti-Sharia law bill has been introduced in the state legislature. Some states have introduced this bill several times while some states have introduced it a few times or not at all. The total number of times the bill has been introduced between 2010 and 2019 serves as the outcome variable in this analysis. The nature of this variable necessitates a Poisson regression approach.

In all cases the analysis is cross-sectional, that is, across states and not across time. Many of the variables included in this analysis variate slightly from year to year which is expected at these aggregated levels. The real variance is between states. In Cox regression the time to an event is an important component in the model and this is how the effect of time is captured in this analysis. This variable has been included in the descriptive statistics in table 8.1. There are also issues with data not available for all variables for all years. For some variables, data are only available for 2010 which is fine since this represents year 0 in the model or the first year of policy adoption. For other variables, there are multiple years of data which can be averaged to produce an overall picture on that variable for that state.

The percentage Muslim and Evangelical variables only have data for 2010. Ideological distance encompasses the entire study period since it is a measure based on policy adoption. The same is true for neighbor adoption. The Squire index was updated in 2015 while the Ranney index includes a moving average from 2007 to 2010. The most important year in that average is 2010, the first year of policy adoption. At the time of this study, the religiosity variable was available for the years 2012–2016, so this was averaged across those years. The education variable was measured at 2010, the last Census at the time of this study.

A cross-sectional analysis at the state-level limits the number of cases to 50. There is a convention in regression that there should be at least 10 cases per variable in order to avoid over-fitting in the model. Even if this convention is discounted, it is still problematic for estimates. In addition, many of the variables included in this analysis are related to each other. For instance, it is quite logical that religiosity is related to the percentage that are Evangelical Christian. Although there were no issues with multicollinearity between the variables i.e. the tolerance values were well above .1 and the variance inflation factors were below 10, it may still be advantageous to create factor scores that capture multiple variables.

A factor analysis determined that there was enough common covariance between religiosity, ideological distance, percent Evangelical, neighbor adoption, and education that a factor score of uncorrelated variance could be produced and assigned to each case. This factor could be labeled as an ideological and religious factor given its composition. A second factor was also produced with the percent Muslim, ideological distance, and education. All variables loaded positively with this factor indicating that there are positive relationships between the size of the Muslim population with the size of the population with Bachelor's degrees and higher and the size of the ideological distance with adopting states. Basically, Muslims are in more educated and less conservative states. This factor could be labeled the cosmopolitan factor. See table 8.2.

One problem with using factor scores instead of the original measures for each of the variables is interpretability. It is difficult to break out the effects of each individual variable on the outcome. One can see the strength of a variable loading in a factor and the direction of that loading which allow some general conclusions about individual effects. In this analysis granularity is sacrificed for greater accuracy.

Table 8.2 Factor Analysis Results

	Ideology & Religion Factor	*Cosmopolitan Factor*
Religiosity	0.896	X
Ideological Distance	-0.779	0.466
% Evangelical	0.771	X
% Neighbor Adopt	0.764	X
% Higher Education	-0.636	0.575
% Muslim	X	0.896

Note: Rotation Method: Varimax with Kaiser Normalization. Factor loadings below .4 not shown. KMO = .772 ($\rho \leq .0001$). Variance explained = 74.2. 66% of nonredundant residuals with values greater than .05.

The causal relationship for the Cox regression is conceptualized in equation 8.1 below. Two separate regressions are considered so that the full sample of states can be included in the analysis. In the separate regression the Ranney index is excluded for this reason. Nebraska is not included in the index because it has a unicameral system of government. This was also done with the logistic and Poisson regressions. The causal relationship for the logistic regression and the Poisson regressions is conceptualized in equations 8.2 and 8.3, respectively.

Equation 8.1

$$Ln\,h(t) = a(t) + b_1 Ideology\ \&\ Religion\ Factor_1 + b_2 Cosmopolitan\ Factor_2 + b_3 \%\ Anti-Muslim_3 + b_4 Squire\ Index_4 + b_5 Ranney\ Index_5$$

Equation 8.2

$$Ln\left[\frac{\rho_i}{1-\rho_i}\right] = b_1 Ideology\ \&\ Religion\ Factor_1 + b_2 Cosmopolitan\ Factor_2 + b_3 \%\ Anti-Muslim_3 + b_4 Squire\ Index_4 + b_5 Ranney\ Index_5$$

Equation 8.3

$$\mu = t\exp\begin{pmatrix} b_1 Ideology\ \&\ Religion\ Factor_1 + b_2 Cosmopolitan\ Factor_2 \\ + b_3 \%\ Anti-Muslim_3 + b_4 Squire\ Index_4 + b_5 Ranney\ Index_5 \end{pmatrix}$$

Harrell's C as well as the model chi-square are used to test for model fit with equation 8.1. Somers' D is used to test for explained variance in this equation. Somers' D is commonly used for this purpose in Cox regression albeit its estimates are considered more conservative than a Pearson's R^2 calculation used in OLS.[5] The model chi-square is used to test for model fit with equation 8.2 while the Nagelkerke R^2 is used to test for explained variance. Similarly, the model chi-square is used to test for model fit with equation 8.3 while the pseudo-R^2 is used to test for explained variance.

STUDY RESULTS

In table 8.3, the results for the Cox regressions are shown. Regression 1 is the full regression with the Ranney index, but with only 49 states (excluding Nebraska). Regression 2 does not have the Ranney index, but has all 50 states. In both regressions, the only significant variable is the ideology and religion factor. This factor is very significant with the largest effect. A 1 unit increase in this factor score increases the odds for having an anti-Sharia law by more than 200 percent. Odds is the probability of an event occurring over it not occurring. This is a major effect, but is influenced by the scale of the factor variable. By design these factors have a variance and standard deviation of 1. A 1 unit increase in this score is a major shift.

As explained in the last section, it is difficult to interpret individual variable effects in a factor score on the outcome. In table 8.2, the variable with the largest influence on the ideology and religion factor is religiosity which loads positively on the factor. This means that an increase in religiosity increases a factor score for a state. By implication, this means that an increase in religiosity increases the odds for a state having an anti-Sharia law. It is the most impactful variable in the factor. The second most impactful variable in that

Table 8.3 Cox Regression Results

	Regression 1 β *(CI)*	*Regression 2* β *(CI)*
Ideology & Religion Factor	3.822* (1.57, 9.3)	3.455* (1.622, 7.363)
Cosmopolitan Factor	0.419 (.150, 1.174)	0.499 (.190, 1.305)
% Anti-Muslim	1.047 (.992, 1.105)	1.042 (.990, 1.095)
Squire Index	88.514 (.018, 41999.4)	14.235 (.004, 55949.7)
Ranney Index	0.303 (.041, 2.23)	X X

Note: Regression 1: *$p \leq .01$, df = 43, N = 49, C = .80; D = .60, Chi-square = 16.237 ($p \leq .01$). | Regression 2: *$p \leq .001$, df = 45, N = 50, C = .79; D = .58, Chi-square = 14.811 ($p \leq .01$).

factor is ideological distance which loads negatively in the score. This would mean that an increase in ideological distance between a state and other adopting states decreases the odds for having an anti-Sharia law. The ideology of focus in that measure is conservatism. A decrease in the number of conservatives in a state decreases the chances of having this law. The percentage Evangelical and neighbor adoption are the third and fourth most impactful variables in the factor, respectively. In both cases an increase in these variables increases the factor score and thereby increases the odds of a state having an anti-Sharia law. In summary, a state with more Evangelicals as a percentage of the total population and with a greater number of adopting neighbors are more likely to have this law. The least impactful variable in the factor, percentage with a higher education, loaded negatively meaning that an increase in the percentage with a Bachelor's degree or higher decreased the factor score and consequently decreased the odds for having an anti-Sharia law in a state.

If one were to develop a profile of an adopting state, it would be states with a greater share of their population that identify as very religious, more conservative, more Evangelical, with a smaller share of the population with higher educations and in a neighborhood where others are adopting the law. The cosmopolitan factor was not significant in either regression in table 8.3. Its effect was also marginal. The variable with the largest impact on that factor was the percent Muslim. Apparently, the presence of Muslims in a state is not important for whether a state has this law.

The other variables included in the regressions were also not significant. This includes the presence of anti-Muslim groups and both the Squire index and Ranney index. This means that religious and ideological factors matter more than political factors or the activism of anti-Muslim groups for whether a state has an anti-Sharia law.

The logistic regression returned similar results as the Cox regression. The only variable that was statistically significant was the ideology and religion factor. The effect was larger than the other variables and in the same direction as the Cox regression. A 1 unit increase in the ideology and religion factor is related to more than a 700 percent increase in the odds of having an anti-Sharia law. These odds increase when the sample size increases with the exclusion of the Ranney index. In terms of probabilities, a 1 unit increase in the ideology and religion factor is related to an 89.5 percent probability of having an anti-Sharia law. This probability increases to 90.1 percent with the full sample of states. Probability is a description of the number of occurrences that is the existence of an anti-Sharia law versus the number of possibilities that is having or not having an anti-Sharia law. See table 8.4. The interpretation of the logistic regression is the same as the Cox regression. The only difference is the size of the effect which is larger with the logistic regression.

When the model is included as a whole including all the other variables, the predicted probability of a state having an anti-Sharia law is 52.6 percent excluding Nebraska. When including Nebraska, and excluding the Ranney index, the predicted probability is 52 percent. This is a marginal difference. This means that given the levels of the variables across the 50 states it is more likely that a state will have an anti-Sharia law then not having one. The probability is slightly greater than chance (50/50). This also means that the variables selected to make this prediction are better at predicting whether a state has this law over chance. The probability of a state not having this law is only 15 percent.

The number of times the bill was introduced (2010–2019) is a different outcome variable with slightly different results. The ideology and religion factor is also significant with this analysis. A 1 unit increase in the factor score is related to a .671 log count increase in the number of anti-Sharia laws introduced in a state. In other words, a 1 unit increase in the factor score is related to a 1.956 increase in the introduction of anti-Sharia bills. That is nearly two more bills. It is slightly more than two when Nebraska is included in the analysis. See table 8.5.

The anti-Muslim and Ranney index variables are significant in this analysis. A 1 unit increase in the percentage of hate groups that are anti-Muslim is related to a .014 log count increase in the introduction of anti-Sharia laws. This is a little more than 1 extra bill introduction. A 1 unit increase in the Ranney index is related to a .506 log count decrease in the number of these bills. This is a decrease in the number of bills by 1.66. The other factor and the Squire index remained insignificant in this analysis.

Table 8.4 Logistic Regression Results

	Regression 1 β *(CI)*	*Regression 2* β *(CI)*
Constant	0.032	0.024
Ideology & Religion Factor	8.5*	9.087*
	(1.921, 37.89)	(2.020, 40.88)
Cosmopolitan Factor	0.407	0.441
	(.112, 1.48)	(.138, 1.407)
% Anti-Muslim	1.055	1.054
	(.979, 1.136)	(.981, 1.133)
Squire Index	401	187.1
	(.011, 14154621)	(.007, 4991519)
Ranney Index	0.389	X
	(.022, 6.77)	X

Note: Regression 1: * $p \leq .01$, df = 43, N = 49, Nagelkerke R^2 = .482, Chi-square = 19.185 ($p \leq .01$). | Regression 2: *$p \leq .01$, df = 45, N = 50, Nagelkerke R^2 = .468, Chi-square = 18.718 ($p \leq .001$).

Table 8.5 Poisson Regression Results

	Regression 1 β *(CI)*	*Regression 2* β *(CI)*
Constant	1.25**	1.089**
	(.764, 1.737)	(.612, 1.566)
Ideology & Religion Factor	.671**	.704**
	(.513, .829)	(.553, .855)
Cosmopolitan Factor	-0.039	-0.02
	(-.183, .106)	(-.161, .122)
% Anti-Muslim	0.014*	0.015*
	(.002, .026)	(.002, .027)
Squire Index	0.512	0.032
	(-1.262, 2.286)	(-1.766, 1.829)
Ranney Index	-0.506*	X
	(-.942, -.070)	X

Note: Regression 1: $*p \leq .05$; $**p \leq .001$, df = 43, N = 49, Pseudo $R^2 = .514$, Chi-square = 111.79 ($p \leq .0001$). | Regression 2: $*p \leq .01$; $**p \leq .001$, df = 45, N = 50, Pseudo $R^2 = .530$, Chi-square = 105.965 ($p \leq .0001$).

The interesting finding with this analysis is the significant effects of the anti-Muslim and Ranney index variables. This analysis shows that the influence of anti-Muslim groups may be limited to encouraging the introduction of these laws, but not their passage. The significance of the Ranney index indicates that as a state becomes more Democratically controlled it is less likely to introduce this law. This could also be due to a lack of political competition with less incentive to score points with a subsector of the electorate.

On average, those states that passed an anti-Sharia law had introduced the bill more than eight times compared to a little more than three times on average for non-adopting states. Even though anti-Muslim groups or the Ranney index were not significantly related to bill adoption, their significant relationship with bill introduction is an important contribution. Anti-Muslim groups lobby for these bills, while more Democratic states avoid them.

DISCUSSION AND CONCLUSION

The analysis in this book confirmed some assumptions while disproving others. The assumption that religious salience matters for whether a state has an anti-Sharia law was confirmed in this analysis. Although measured through the factor score, given its dominant position in that score and the significance of the factor, it is one of the most significant findings. The United States remains a religious country when compared to other Western countries. As discussed throughout this book, religion has been an important aspect of the culture. Religious liberty was so important to the founders of the nation that the First Amendment of the Constitution guarantees it. The passage of anti-Sharia laws is a contradiction to this and is only understood when religious salience is analyzed in connection to debates over Islam in America. Is Islam a religion? The only people seriously pondering that question are nationalists and fundamentalists. Muslims are seen as deviant possibly because their religion refutes many of the core theological tenants of Christianity. This is beside the point that Muslims and Christians share more in common than other faith communities.[6] They are also predominantly people of color which irks some nationalists who envision America as a White Judeo-Christian nation.

The other variables in that factor are also interesting contributors. The size of the Evangelical community and ideological distance seem the most related to religious salience. Religious believers tend to be conservative and Evangelicals are known for their religiosity. It should be noted that not every person that is religious, conservative, and Evangelical is Islamophobic, but this analysis has uncovered a possible relationship between these variables and the introduction and adoption of anti-Sharia laws. As explained there are branches of Evangelical Christianity with the fundamentalist branch being the most predispositioned toward Islamophobic beliefs. Conservatives are also not all the same as explained in the book. Some conservatives are focused on fiscal and economic matters, while others are focused on moral issues which they have in common with Muslims and actively work with them on these issues. Other conservatives are more nationalistic mostly born out of the Cold War and it is these conservatives that tend to be more Islamophobic.

As expected, education loaded negatively on the ideology and religion factor. People who have higher education tend to be less religious and ideologically driven in the United States. Naturally, it would be expected that they would balk at anti-Sharia laws and any suggestion that Islam is not a religion or Muslims do not deserve the same rights as everyone else. To an educated person the very notion of granting rights to some while denying it to others undermines the entire principles of the Constitution and the nation. This is the reason the civil rights movement battled for a century in order to hold the country to this standard.

The insignificance of the cosmopolitan factor or the factor that included the percentage Muslim in a state is also an interesting finding. It was assumed that as the Muslim population grew there would either be more contact that would temper Islamophobic feelings or the Muslim population would exert electoral pressures that would prevent the passage of these laws. It was also assumed that adversarial relations could increase as the Muslim population grew leading to more Islamophobic feelings. Either way, the assumption was that there would be a significant effect on whether a state had a law and/or the number of times the bill was introduced in a state.

The insignificance of the Squire index was also not anticipated since it was assumed that an increase in professionalism in the state legislature would reduce the likelihood of a state having the law and/or introducing the law. These variables along with all the other variables were not significant predictors in whether a state had a law with the exception of the ideology and religion factor. This analysis has shown that some of these variables are important for the introduction of these laws, but not as important for whether a state ends up adopting it. This includes the anti-Muslim hate group's variable and the Ranney index which were significantly related to the introduction of these laws, but not their adoption.

One of the takeaways from this analysis is the centrality of religion and ideology to the introduction and passage of these laws. States with higher levels of religiosity, with more shared conservative ideology, with a larger population of Evangelical Christians, with a smaller population that has a higher education and in a neighborhood with adopting states are more likely to introduce this law and adopt it. This was the assumption in the book and the analysis confirmed it.

Another takeaway is the relative unimportance of the size of the Muslim population in a state. On the whole, states that are adopting these laws have a smaller Muslim population than states that are not adopting them. This means that group threat is likely not playing a role in motivating bill introduction or adoption. It could always be a perceived group threat, but not based on the actual presence of Muslims.

An additional and related takeaway is the potential influence of anti-Muslim hate groups. The size of the presence did not matter in the model estimates for law adoption, but it did matter for law introduction. As discussed in this book, these policy entrepreneurs are invested in the passage of these bills and will claim there is a threat of a Muslim takeover with Sharia creeping into the courts and laws of the state. Their influence in motivating lawmakers to introduce these bills seem obvious beyond the analysis in this book since many of these laws follow the wording of the model legislation drafted by these groups.

A final takeaway is the significance of the Ranney index for bill introduction. More Democratic states are less likely to introduce these laws. This is an assumption in this book as Islam is part of the political culture war with Democrats more likely to defend the rights of Muslims. Another interpretation is that states with less political competition are less likely to introduce these laws. These laws may serve a purpose i.e. galvanize the electorate in order to secure more votes which may be more important in politically divided states.

This analysis has expanded knowledge on which states are adopting these laws and the possible reasons. Further research is needed to understand why individual legislators voted for these bills. This would require a more qualitative approach such as through interviews with these legislators. These results highlight the importance of religiosity and ideology in promoting these laws. This provides further evidence that Islam is a major concern for religious conservatives who may be promoting a vision of America that is more Christian and less Muslim. This is not unique to the United States as similar movements can be found in Europe although these movements are more focused on the secular aspects of identity with a heavy emphasis on race. These are troubling trends especially as the Muslim population grows and the United States becomes increasingly more diverse.

NOTES

1. Klarner, Carl. "Other Scholars? Competitiveness Measures." Harvard Dataverse. Last modified September 10, 2013. https://dataverse.harvard.edu/dataset.xhtml?persistentId=doi:10.7910/DVN/QSDYLH.
2. Squire, Peverill. 2017. "A Squire Index Update." *State Politics & Policy Quarterly 17*, no. 4, 361–371.
3. Mitchell, Joshua L., and Brendan Toner. 2016. "Exploring the Foundations of US State-Level Anti-Sharia Initiatives." *Politics and Religion 9*, no. 4, 720–743.
4. Allison, Paul P. 1984. *Event History Analysis: Regression for Longitudinal Event Data*. Newbury Park, CA: Sage Publications, 35.
5. Schemper, Michael, and Janez Stare. 1996. "Explained Variation In Survival Analysis." *Statistics in Medicine 15*, no. 19, 1999–2012.
6. Hummel, Daniel. 2017. *Jesus and Muhammad: Commonalities of Two Great Religions*. Tughra Books.

Chapter 9

Conclusions

Religion is important in society even in secular ones like the United States. Many of the core societal values, virtues, and norms have sources within religion. Secularization has created a veil between these values, virtues and norms with religion, but the connections remain nonetheless. This is not necessarily a negative thing. Religion is a motivator to act often times selflessly for others. The values stressed in religion emphasize the community and others over the self, which provides an important balance in an individualistic society like the United States. Self-regulation and control are also important factors in religion which reduce the social costs from excess and the need to enforce law and order. Religion forms bonds between people which creates networks of support. Support and belongingness are important aspects of individual mental health.

Religion provides answers to existential questions while providing purpose to its followers. The answers to these questions also help people to navigate the various stressors in life. The last two decades of the twenty-first century has been an uncertain and tumultuous time. Major economic and public health crises have defined this period making religion even more salient for some people.

These crises can bring out the best or worst in people. Religion can help focus these energies toward building social capital and increasing social consciousness. Naturally, this would increase the number of people willing to help others during these crises. Volunteerism would increase during austere times. Interestingly, volunteerism has declined in the United States during these last two decades.[1] Does this have anything to do with declines in religiosity?

Religion is still seen as a vehicle for fostering civic virtues. Volunteering in church-led functions like a food bank is considered laudable and an example of good citizenship. The National Day of Prayer is observed each year by the Federal government in which the President is required by law to sign a proclamation encouraging all people within the United States to pray on this day. The assumption is that a good legislator is also a God-conscious one. For example, Nancy Pelosi, the current Speaker of the House, who is a Democrat, prays for the President all the time. She felt it necessary to share this at a press conference. If this was not considered a virtue, why share it?[2]

Unfortunately, as explored in this book, religion also creates in-groups and out-groups. This can lead to prejudice toward members of out-groups. In a multicultural society like the United States this is problematic if the goal is to create a cohesive society. Arguments that the United States is a Christian country are both inaccurate and problematic for that reason. There is nothing in any of the founding documents that indicate this is the case. Quite the opposite, the establishment of religion is strictly prohibited by the government. Declaring the country a Christian country naturally excludes other groups who are very much a part of that country. As explored in this book, Muslims have been a part of that country for some time.

The Constitution has secured religious freedom for all people since its ratification. It is a central right in the country and a human right in the world. The lack of religious freedom naturally creates conflict.[3] The complication in the United States and other secular societies is knowing the boundaries of religious freedom. Most people in the United States today, religious and otherwise, support the separation of government and religion. This does not mean that religious values do not influence thoughts on legislation.

The boundaries of religious freedom are constantly being tested by religious believers. Needless to say, religious freedom in the United States is as important as it is controversial. Religious freedom cases are regularly considered by the Supreme Court, the lower courts, and throughout the states. Despite this, religious freedom is unequally applied with the disadvantage to minority faiths. In particular, the focus of this book, the Muslim faith. Efforts to brand Islam as a political movement and not a religion and the fact that these arguments are being heard in courts of law should be disturbing to anyone who celebrates religious freedom as a core right.

These efforts are also connected to efforts to forbid Sharia through legislation. In order to understand the prevalence of this legislation one needs to understand that religion influences public policy. Legislators and bureaucrats alike are aware of the confluence of religious values, public policy, and public management. Despite Constitutional regulations on the establishment of religion, policymakers regularly use religious language to promote the moral imperatives of the government. Often times, these moral imperatives are based within empirical facts on an identified need. Increasingly complex problems with little empirical foundation in support of any particular solution are open to interpretation sometimes based within faith. When religious language is used to support empirically supported solutions the effort is to establish support for the legislation. When the policy is based almost entirely within a faith-based perspective, the association is even more genuine and gathers more support from religious believers. These laws also happen to be much more controversial given the varied interpretations on the issue. This, of course, has nothing to say about policies that do not seem to address any particular problem or there is disagreement on whether it is a problem in the first place. One could easily argue that there is no problem with Sharia in the United States.

As discussed in this book and found in the analysis, religious salience is a major factor in predicting attitudes toward Muslims. An increase in religiosity could predict more anti-Muslim views. This is almost certainly due to the competing theologies between Islam and Christianity. They are two missionary faiths attempting to call others to them. Christians claim the Trinity and Jesus as the, "way and the truth and the life."[4] Muslims on the other hand reject the Trinity[5] and claim that Muhammad is the "last of the prophets."[6]

Religious salience also informed discrimination against the followers of Joseph Smith and what would become known as the Church of Jesus Christ of Latter-Day Saints (LDS). Historically, in Christian Europe, it informed prejudicial attitudes toward Jews as they were collectively blamed for the death of Jesus.[7] As one became more religious they saw non-Christian groups as threatening to their belief system. This broad generalization does not apply to everyone, of course. Many have found that their increased faith has made them more compassionate to others including those not of their faith.

An increase in religiosity increases the prevalence of religion in public policy. It is also seen as a means to provide cohesion in society. Absent an effort to emphasize commonalities between different cultural groups, multiculturalism makes it harder to achieve that cohesion especially if the different cultural groups have different religions. The presence of one of these cultural groups may seem threatening to other cultural groups even if that threat is based only within a narrative. As seen in the analysis in this book, Muslims do not even have to be present to elicit this reaction. The type of thinking that evolves is zero-sum which may explain why people can simultaneously celebrate religious freedom while supporting religious freedom restrictions on Muslims. It is not about procedural fairness as much as it is about viewing the society from the narrow perspective of their faith. Their faith binds them to their community and as they engage with government this guides their perspective. There is no room for outsiders unless these outsiders adhere to their faith and practices. One can see how damaging this perspective is in diverse settings, but it is hard to imagine restrictions on Muslim religious freedom unless this is how people view their society.

The lack of perceived commonality between these groups has led some to try to focus only on establishing an environment in which a free market can thrive absent external threats. This is a libertarian perspective. Voltaire, an eighteenth century French writer, recognized how a morally diverse place could form a cohesive whole through the market. In one of his letters he observed, "Take a view of the Royal Exchange in London, a place more venerable than many courts of justice, where the representatives of all nations meet for the benefit of mankind. There the Jew, the Mahometan, and the Christian transact together, as though they all professed the same religion, and give the name infidel to none, but bankrupts."[8] In this observation, Voltaire asserts that through trade the different religious communities are focused on what binds them, acquiring wealth.

This perspective still lacks a fulfillment of mythos-thinking that is the establishment of emotional connections with others through common values, virtues, and norms. The lack of government involvement in the affairs of religious communities sounds appealing, but it largely means that those religious communities will live apart from other religious communities. They would meet to exchange goods and services, but that would be the extent of the interaction. Similar to extreme individualism, extreme communalism would also detract from the cohesiveness of the society. It should be pointed out that in some societies this state of affairs is assumed to be the only option. This is known as consociationalism in which the groups operate semi-autonomously with an equal power-sharing arrangement. The United States does not operate on this model.

Instead, there is a competition between groups over legislation. Groups form coalitions and amass resources to support their causes. Normally, this is considered an optimal state of affairs. This becomes problematic when this competition is over the granting or removing of rights from other groups. As these disadvantages accrue to a particular group these naturally spread to other groups and ultimately raise fundamental questions over the very rights themselves.

Despite its corrosive nature to the common ground, identity politics will continue to play a role across the nation. Different identity groups will cooperate to further each other's rights while retaining their distinctness as a group with their own beliefs and values. Common humanity identity politics, often lauded as reinforcing the common ground, is largely a convenience of dominant groups. Minority groups like Muslims in the United States are unlikely to adopt this perspective on a wide scale when the validity of their existence is being questioned by the dominant groups. However, in order to create a harmonious society, there should be more stress on a common humanity. This will require the dominant group to recognize their oppression and end it. The problem is the dominant group either ignores this oppression or argues that it's not a problem.

American Muslims have been attempting to find this common ground for some time. This has led to arguments that Islam has the same roots as other religions with similar values and beliefs. The interfaith movement is part of this effort. Unfortunately, this perspective is rejected by traditional conservatives who argue that Islam is completely different than Christianity and its values foreign and unacceptable in the Western world. Even worse, some of these conservatives allege that Muslims are engaging in *taqiyya* or lying about their religion when drawing these parallels. When confronted with this outright rejection, it is unlikely that a common humanity perspective will flourish between these opposing groups. In response, American Muslims have been attempting to form a solidified voting bloc while working together with other groups that suffer from similar oppressions. These developments can be described in no other way than identity politics.

Rights cannot be applied to one group and denied to another one. That defeats the purpose of having rights in the first place. There are two directions one can go with these liberties. Increasingly, the circle could expand encompassing more groups in an effort to be as inclusive as possible. The circle could contract narrowly focusing on granting rights to specific groups. Ultimately, this would lead to lawsuits from excluded groups with little recourse but to either expand these rights or contract them for the privileged group.

The unequal application of rights has led to communal discord. The unequal treatment of North Africans in France led to the riots in 2005 and that same year in Cronulla by the Arab population in Australia. There is a history of riots in the United States over similar issues with the African American population. These riots laid bare the glaring inequality and prejudicial treatment toward these minority populations. It also showed that these injustices will cause more unrest in the future.

Discomfort over their Muslim populations has led to grievous atrocities in the last five years around the world leading to more unrest. Consider the genocide perpetuated against the Rohingya Muslims of Myanmar or the Muslims in the Central African Republic. Although the scale of this violence and unrest is unlikely in the United States in the twenty-first century, other outcomes can be just as troublesome. Discrimination in employment, the shutting down of Muslim charities, imprisonment of Muslims over flawed charges and the banning of Muslims from certain countries are alienating Muslim Americans. This is problematic if the goal is to create a cohesive country out of disparate parts.

Muslims have been in the United States for a long time, but their place in the country has always been controversial.[9] In the 1960s when the immigration laws were liberalized allowing more Muslim immigration along with the conversion of many African Americans to Islam, the number of Muslims in the country expanded beyond their previous levels. Naturally, this increased conflict with the dominant religious communities.

To put this in perspective, Islam is the second largest religion in many states while it is projected to be the second largest religion nationwide by the middle of the twenty-first century.[10] Limitations on free exercise and wide scale prejudice toward Muslims in America affects millions of Americans. At the time of this study, the size of the Muslim population is not significantly related to the introduction or passage of anti-Sharia laws. This may change with an increase in the Muslim population.

The negative effect of anti-Muslim discrimination is particularly burdensome for Muslim youth. A study surveyed Muslim young adults in Genesee County, Michigan on their experiences with discrimination. The Muslim population has increased by more than 400 percent in this county making it one of the top 100 counties in the country for Muslims as a percentage of the total population. The percentage of Muslims there is 2.6 percent as of 2010. This is well above the average of 1.1 percent that same year. Despite these numbers, Muslim youth experience different forms of discrimination. It was found that these Muslim youth sometimes experience hearing anti-Arab and anti-Muslim rhetoric and are sometimes accused of doing something wrong even when they have not done anything. This last form of discrimination is very damaging and has been given different names in the Muslim community that mirror the experiences in the African American community. Terms like "guilt by association" and "flying while Muslim" have become common to explain the attitudes toward Muslims and the assumption that they are doing something wrong. It was also found that this form of discrimination has significantly impacted the propensity of these Muslim youth to identify as Americans. This shows that discrimination negatively affects social cohesion in the United States.[11]

Forty-four percent of the respondents to the survey mentioned religion or religious identity as the reason they experience unfair treatment. One participant stated, "I believe I am treated unfairly due to my appearance and the fact that I can clearly be identified as a Muslim woman. I also believe this unfair treatment is related to my religion." Some described being treated unfairly due to their religious identity and that often they experience this unfair treatment due to wearing religious clothing such as a hijab or kufi. They also stated that they are treated unfairly due to their religion because of stereotypes about Muslims. One participant stated, "I've only been treated unfairly due to my heritage and religion. People believe Muslims are bad people who represent bad things."[12]

Some of the Muslim youth also shared their stress battling anti-Muslim stereotypes. They discussed the impacts of these stereotypes including in the workplace and the portrayal of Muslims in the media. One individual wrote, "I believe it is related to my religion and the biases some may have toward Muslims due to media and opinions of public figures."[13]

The results of this survey in a robust Muslim community in Michigan, a state which almost elected the first Muslim governor, has many Muslim state representatives, and one of the first Muslim women serving in Congress, is troubling for the future of community relations. Michigan does not have an anti-Sharia law, but it has introduced the law four times between 2011 and 2017 which is average for the states. Clearly, there is a problem with Islamophobia in Michigan. This is evident in a statement by Kalkaska Village President, Jeff Sieting, who posted on social media that every Muslim should be killed.[14] This is not subtle anti-Muslim attitudes where prejudicial actions against Muslims are clouded behind a veil of false equivalence and seemingly unbiased reasons for terminating a Muslim employee, for example. This is overt calls for violence against Muslims that mirror similar calls in places like Myanmar.[15]

Hateful statements like these need to be actively challenged by everyone in society. Silence is seen as complicity. These attitudes did not appear over night, but are a culmination of decades of discourse around Islam and Muslims in the United States. Islamophobia or the fear and hatred of Islam has been a problem across political spectrums; however, traditional conservatives in the 1990s were critical in transforming orientalism to Islamophobia. Whether it was the work of Samuel Huntington[16] or Bernard Lewis,[17] Islam was envisioned as the next big threat to the West following the collapse of the Soviet Union. These scholars along with a multitude of ideologues laid the groundwork for a post-9/11 anti-Muslim backlash and the global "War on Terror." It should be pointed out that this narrative is so pervasive that when terror attacks are perpetuated by non-Muslims there is a resistance to labeling them as such.[18]

Islamophobia is about stereotyping Muslims and framing them as outsiders attacking the West. Historical symbols are conjured from the Crusades in order to make the argument that this is a historical and existential fight between the West and Islam. Muslims in the West are considered a "fifth column" who need to be regularly monitored at the very least and expelled if possible.

Islamophobia, which was born of orientalism, also overlaps with general racism and xenophobia. Most Muslims are people of color making the association of Islam with them easier. Since Islam is not a "race," racism can be masked within Islamophobic discourse. Since Muslims are often framed as outsiders, anti-immigrant sentiments are also wrapped in this discourse.

The imperative to protect the "homeland" from Muslim threats may mean a reduction of the people of color in a community. The anti-immigrant sentiment in the United States often discusses the southern border as a backdoor for terrorists. There have been false claims about Muslim prayer rugs found at the border as an example.[19]

One of the fault lines in this conflict is the anti-Sharia laws, the focus of this book. Sharia is not well understood by the average American. It is typically understood by references to some form of capital punishments exhibited in Afghanistan or Saudi Arabia. Gender relations is also a central talking point regarding Sharia including things as innocuous as dress codes to more serious attributions like the concept of "honor killing." Arguments on the existence of capital punishments in Islamic law are a paper tiger argument since many of these same punishments are described in the Bible. As explained in this book, Sharia is more fluid than assumed with wide-ranging interpretations. Despite this, Sharia is a central aspect of Islam and its banning raises existential questions about the place of Muslims in the United States. Even if the laws are unenforceable, which in some cases they have been enforced in the civil courts, the symbolic impacts of the laws are isolating to the Muslim American population.

Muslim Americans fear the erosion of their religious liberties such as how they dress, what they eat and how they pray. They also rely on Islamic law for marriage, divorce, inheritance and other areas related to the family. Education is a central aspect of this as Islamic schools would be under threat in a state with an anti-Sharia law. Their curriculum could be called into question by a judge implementing one of these laws. The same could be said of mosques where the rules of Islam are enforced in different matters. Muslim cemeteries would fall under additional scrutiny since the burial practices are based on Islamic law. Basically, every aspect of practice in Islam could potentially be challenged in court. The end result could be the elimination of everything deemed Islamic except for nominal recognition. You could call yourself a Muslim, but not practice Islam. Given what is known about the importance of religion to people this would be an unacceptable outcome.

These laws originate entirely within conservative circles. Some religious communities have been proponents of the laws including the Evangelical Christian community. Previous research on these laws considered ideology and religious affiliation, but not religious salience. The analysis in this book considered religiosity as a unique factor in the introduction and passing of these laws. As of the writing of this book, 12 states have passed some form of an anti-Sharia law. As predicted, religiosity mattered the most for bill introduction and adoption. According to the analysis in this book, religious zeal motivates action against Islam. As with any statistical analysis, there are limitations based on the methodology, sample, and selected controls.

However, these results confirm the theory developed in this book on the relationship between religious salience and Islamophobia.

The presence of anti-Muslim groups in a state also mattered for bill introduction. Theoretically, these groups are expected to frame the narrative on Islam and Muslims through the lobbying of state legislators and information campaigns. These groups have been known to put ads on buses, for example. They may also visit churches and other houses of worship to spread their cause among those most likely to listen to it. In turn, these people will go on to pressure their legislators to support the adoption of an anti-Sharia law. These organizations may also stage high profile events like protests in order to perpetuate a negative image of the Muslim community in the state.

On the other side of the scale, education and more Democratic states decreased the probability of introducing and/or passing one of these laws. A more educated population decreases the likelihood of introducing the law in the first place let alone passing one. Those who are educated may see these laws as mostly symbolic yet highly controversial that is these laws introduce significant costs (increased litigation and the alienation of sections of the population) with little benefit. In addition, more educated people may either know Muslims or have studied Islam in college reducing fear and hatred of it.

Education could also ameliorate extreme positions and prejudicial attitudes toward Muslims and others. The analysis in this book confirmed the association between education and a decreased probability of introducing anti-Sharia laws. The benefits from education for building a prosperous and stable society have been known since the founding of the nation. This is why state constitutions guarantee the right to education even though this is not explicitly mentioned in the US Constitution.[20]

The problem is that education is one of the major expenditure categories for state governments following healthcare. Unlike healthcare spending, the state has many options for making cuts to education by pushing this spending down on local governments and private funders.[21] The result has been a continual decline in education spending by state governments which has put considerable stress upon systems of higher education in these states.[22] In some states like Michigan, this has involved "robbing Peter to pay Paul" with funds allocated for secondary education being reallocated to higher education.[23] The K–12 schools are also suffering from budget cuts and it is one of the reasons that teachers remain underpaid for their services with many teachers with great potential seeking careers in other fields leading to teacher shortages.[24] Along with state budget cuts brought about by the COVID-19 virus lock down, many universities are cutting faculty, staff, and administrators who are responsible for delivering these services.[25] The end result of all of this could be a decreased quality of education and limited access to higher education.

Ultimately, this could increase societal tensions along with a decrease in prosperity. Tolerance for those that are different from them could also decline with a greater incidence of laws like the anti-Sharia laws. For some, this is a positive turn of events. For example, Republicans have been uncomfortable with higher education for some time.[26] They see it as an institution of indoctrination for liberal values. Those liberal values such as equality that might lead one to reject an anti-Sharia law would be seen as an effort to create a moral equivalency between Islam and the West. This is rejected on the political Right and even though religious freedom is a celebrated right among conservatives they applaud efforts to limit the freedoms of Muslims. In contrast, those on the political Right are interested in their own version of indoctrination. For example, in some states there has been an effort to have more lessons on Islam and Islamic civilization like there are lessons on other faiths and civilizations in K–12 schools. People were uncomfortable with this because it might show Islam in a "good light." Some state boards of education capitulated and removed all references to Islam from the curriculum.[27] Those on the political Right will only accept negative portrayals of the faith or its complete erasure from the discussion. Naturally, anti-Muslim attitudes will flourish in this environment with a greater propensity to pass Islamophobic legislation.

Education is an important tool for boosting critical thinking skills. The age of information overload has weakened abilities to discern factual information from falsehoods. Social media has played a significant role in spreading falsehoods. This coupled with poor educational outcomes has increased extremism in the United States. Rumors about "Sharia courts" in the United States,[28] Islamberg in upstate New York[29] and "no-go zones"[30] have proliferated on the internet leading to extremist violence against Muslim communities. Unfortunately, these rumors perpetuated on the internet from its far corners have found their way onto major news networks like Fox News. Fox News for years peddled in Islamophobic discourse and only recently backpedaled when Jeanine Pirro made extreme anti-Muslim comments on her show.[31] Fox News has been described as a mouthpiece for the Republican Party.

Although seemingly beneficial for their reelection, the Republican Party should distance itself from Islamophobic rhetoric and individuals especially those on the far right who are part of the alt-right or alt-light. Electoral strategies based on racism, bigotry and xenophobia work in the short-term, but not in the long-term. This is especially the case as the demographics change in the country. According to projections, the United States will be "minority White" by 2045.[32] This may also explain why the popular vote for president has favored Democrats over Republicans.[33] The hurdle is the electoral system, but internal migration may change this over time. The middle part of the country, which has traditionally voted Republican with many electoral votes, is increasingly appealing to young, educated professionals looking for an affordable place to live. The movement of many jobs online especially in the face of the pandemic will make place even less relevant. Islamophobic rhetoric will not appeal to these voters.

States under more Democratic control are less likely to introduce anti-Sharia laws. As explored in this book, the measure selected (Ranney index) is a measure of political competition. A state under Democratic control has less political competition than a state in the middle between Republican and Democratic control. Even though this is the purpose of the measure, it is more plausible that it has more to do with which political party is in control of the state. Most of the states that have passed these laws are under the control of the Republican Party and none of these laws have been introduced by Democratic lawmakers. Islam and these laws in particular have been a partisan issue. Democrats typically view Islam and Muslims as part of the fabric of the country. The disparaging things said about Muslims especially by those on the political Right are a target of repudiation by those on the political Left.

Both Democrats and Republicans should also refrain from engaging in patriotism tests of Muslim Americans. This is not expected of other groups and only creates dissatisfaction in the Muslim American community. In addition, Democrats should avoid assuming they are "woke" on the issue of Islamophobia. There are myriad experiences with discrimination in the Muslim community with different interpretations on how best to address it. Well-meaning people on the political Left could end up hurting this community. They should also stop using Islam and Muslims as a "culture war" issue in their battles with those on the political Right.

Besides changing the way politicians speak about Islam and the Muslim community, religious leaders have a role in abetting this hateful rhetoric. As a nation that still respects religious leaders and attends religious functions at a much higher rate than other Western developed nations, religious leaders can exacerbate this problem or abate it. This will require religious leaders to put communal harmony above theological disagreements and efforts to create in-groups and out-groups. The ability to do this will determine the future of the nation.

Much of this is about how we communicate with each other. The problems of Islamophobia are compounded by the way we communicate today. Social media has democratized the flow of information. People can share directly with a wide audience their thoughts and experiences and what they believe is the truth. Even those that reject the notion of "truth" see social media as a marketplace of ideas that can be sold like any other good. Only those goods that have value that is good ideas can survive these exchanges, at least this is the argument.

Much has been argued on the "wisdom of crowds" and the idea that people are smarter as a group.[34] Social media has complicated this notion. People produce content for online consumption with some people making a living at it. The way that information is shared on these platforms is through virality. For information to "go viral" it needs to activate emotions in which the most powerful emotions are either joy or rage.[35] This has led some to use these emotions in order to build their social media profile and get followers. The exchange in truthful information has become less important than exchanging emotionally activating information whether it's true or not. As long as it's plausible often times by confirming stereotypes the information goes viral.

Normally, politicians and media outlets, traditional gate-keepers, would dispel false information. The relevancy of these gate-keepers has decreased over the years with some media outlets and politicians using this activating information online to drive readers and voters in their direction. People in positions of power are known as "influencers" and when they share online content the spread of the information increases substantially as it gains legitimacy.[36] There is no greater influencer than the former President of the United States, Donald Trump, who was quite active on social media (before he was banned) and had shared questionable material on his accounts with clear anti-Muslim messages.[37]

Andrew Marantz wrote about these social media influencers and decided that, "… taken together they'd had a decisive impact on the 2016 campaign, and on public opinion more broadly. It was hard to imagine Trump winning without them."[38] Trump's virulent anti-Muslim campaign culminating in the Muslim Ban helped to bolster support for his election. Many online social media influencers are solidly anti-Muslim and use Islamophobia to increase their number of followers. In Trump they found the ultimate influencer and voice for their cause.

In his work, Marantz described their efforts as focused on shifting the "Overton window." This is a reference to a libertarian think tank in the 1990s that described how cultural vocabularies change over time with the center of the "window" being the mainstream and the fringes being marginal ideas.[39] The goal is to bring the fringes to the mainstream. This is done through the marketplace of ideas and primarily through social media in today's environment. The goal is not the discovery of truth, but the shifting of the narrative as Marantz observed, "there is no such thing as a society without a Narrative; there are only better Narratives and worse ones."[40] The struggle over narrative seems to be constant in society and which narratives become mainstream have less to do about the "wisdom of the crowd" and more about which activate the most emotions.

According to Bail, fringe anti-Muslim groups present a socially attractive narrative full with raw and negative emotion.[41] The emotion is rage/anger combined with fear, which are strong activating emotions. This message has found an audience through social media and has drifted into the mainstream in the government, the media, and public opinion. This pull toward the extremes was observed by Taleb who argued that extremist positions influence the whole. He described this process as renormalizing.[42] Increasingly, Muslims have been dehumanized into a monolithic threat to anyone who is not Muslim. This has led to dangerous conclusions that some have openly advocated for, but most avoid because of its implications.

When the possibility of putting Muslims in camps was brought up, the claim is dismissed as if this has not happened in the United States with other groups. Some refer to this as a "straw man argument" which distorts their claims that the West faces a real threat from Islam and that they have a duty to "say it as they see it." One may wonder if this was the type of discourse that led up to the Spanish expulsion of Muslims and Jews during the Reconquista, noted as Europe's first genocide, or the Holocaust in the twentieth century, Europe's worst genocide. What about Europe's latest genocide against the Bosnian Muslims?

Before that genocide, one of the architects Radovan Karadžić, openly said the Muslims will disappear. One could dismiss this statement as posturing in order to secure support from one's base, in this case Serb nationalists. One could easily dismiss the Muslim Ban in the United States in the same way. Dismissing this discourse as simply words or politics without serious ramifications is a mistake. It has real world consequences. Ask the Muslims in Christchurch, New Zealand when a gunman killed more than 50 worshippers while he livestreamed it on social media. Tarrant, the shooter, was inspired by Radovan.

The anti-Sharia movement has shown that whether or not there are open discussions and advocacy for genocide, being Muslim in the United States makes one an outsider and not welcome in the eyes of some. As the fringe organizations that advocate for these positions move into the mainstream one can only speculate on future public policy. For the sake of creating a cohesive society, these policies should be vigorously opposed so that all feel welcome in the United States.

NOTES

1. Poon, Linda. 2019. "Why Americans Stopped Volunteering." CityLab. Last modified September 17, 2019. https://www.citylab.com/life/2019/09/volunteer-opportunities-charitable-giving-national-service/597856/.

2. Luo, Michael. 2019. "'I Pray for the President All the Time': In Praise of How Nancy Pelosi Has Navigated Impeachment." *The New Yorker*, December 17, 2019.

https://www.newyorker.com/news/daily-comment/i-pray-for-the-president-all-the-time-in-praise-of-how-nancy-pelosi-has-navigated-impeachment.

3. Finke, Roger, and Robert R. Martin. 2013. "Religious Freedom and Conflict A Review of the Evidence." Association of Religion. Last modified October 11, 2013. https://blogs.thearda.com/trend/primers-tutorials/religious-freedom-and-conflict-a-review-of-the-evidence-by-roger-finke-and-robert-r-martin/.

4. John 14:6.

5. Surah An-Nisa: 171.

6. Surah Al-Ahzab: 40.

7. Rohrbacher, Stefan. 1991. "The charge of deicide. An anti-Jewish motif in medieval Christian art." *Journal of Medieval History 17*, no. 4, 297–321.

8. Voltaire, François. 2015. "Letter VI-On the Presbyterians. Voltaire, François Marie Arouet De. 1909–14. Letters on the English. The Harvard Classics." Homework Help and Textbook Solutions | Bartleby. Last modified 2015. https://www.bartleby.com/34/2/6.html.

9. GhaneaBassiri, Kambiz. 2010. *A History of Islam in America: From the New World to the New World Order*. Cambridge: Cambridge University Press.

10. "Data Archive." The Association of Religion Data Archives | Quality Data on Religion. Last modified 2020. https://www.thearda.com/; AJ Willingham, CNN. "By 2040, Islam Could Be the Second-largest Religion in the US." CNN. Last modified January 11, 2018. https://www.cnn.com/2018/01/10/politics/muslim-population-growth-second-religious-group-trnd/index.html.

11. Hummel, Daniel, Mohamed Daassa, Nuha Alshabani, and Leen Felo. "Identifying as Muslim and American: The Role of Discrimination." *Review of Religious Research*, forthcoming.

12. Ibid.

13. Ibid.

14. Gmiter, Tanda. "Michigan Official Stands by Call for Killing All Muslims." Mlive. Last modified July 12, 2017. https://www.mlive.com/news/2017/07/michigan_official_stands_by_ca.html.

15. Keane, Fergal. "Meeting Myanmar's Hardline Buddhist Monks." BBC News. Last modified September 14, 2017. https://www.bbc.com/news/world-asia-41263073.

16. Huntington, Samuel P. 1993. "The Clash of Civilizations?" *Foreign Affairs 72*, no. 3, 22–49.

17. Lewis, Bernard. 1990. "The Roots of Muslim Rage." *The Atlantic.*

18. Yin, Tung. 2013. "Were Timothy McVeigh and the unabomber the only white terrorists?: Race, religion, and the perception of terrorism." *Alabama Civil Rights & Civil Liberties Law Review 4*, 1–50.

19. Ohlheiser, Abby, and Lindsey Bever. "How an old, far-right meme about Muslim 'prayer rugs' at the border became a Trump tweet." *Washington Post* (Washington), January 18, 2019. https://www.washingtonpost.com/technology/2019/01/18/how-an-old-far-right-meme-about-muslim-prayer-rugs-border-became-trump-tweet/.

20. Zackin, Emily. 2013. *Looking for Rights in All the Wrong Places: Why State Constitutions Contain America's Positive Rights*. Princeton: Princeton University Press.

21. Boylan, Richard T., and Vivian Ho. 2017. "The Most Unkindest Cut of All? State Spending on Health, Education, and Welfare During Recessions." *National Tax Journal 70*, no. 2, 329–366.

22. Mitchell, Michael, Michael Leachman, and Matthew Saenz. "State Higher Education Funding Cuts Have Pushed Costs to Students, Worsened Inequality." Center on Budget and Policy Priorities. Last modified November 15, 2019. https://www.cbpp.org/research/state-budget-and-tax/state-higher-education-funding-cuts-have-pushed-costs-to-students.

23. Ruark, Peter. "A Hard Habit to Break: The Raiding of K-12 Funds for Postsecondary Education." MLPP. Last modified February 22, 2019. https://mlpp.org/budget-issues/a-hard-habit-to-break-the-raiding-of-k-12-funds-for-postsecondary-education/.

24. Walker, Tim. "Teacher Shortage is 'Real and Growing, and Worse Than We Thought.'" NEA Today. Last modified April 12, 2019. https://neatoday.org/2019/04/03/how-bad-is-the-teacher-shortage/.

25. Flaherty, Colleen. "Professors at Ohio U Say Faculty Cuts Can't Just Be Blamed on COVID-19." Inside Higher Ed | Higher Education News, Career Advice, Jobs. Last modified May 5, 2020. https://www.insidehighered.com/news/2020/05/05/professors-ohio-u-say-faculty-cuts-cant-just-be-blamed-covid-19.

26. Kreighbaum, Andrew. "Majority of Republicans Have Negative View of Higher Ed, Pew Finds." Inside Higher Ed | Higher Education News, Career Advice, Jobs. Last modified August 20, 2019. https://www.insidehighered.com/news/2019/08/20/majority-republicans-have-negative-view-higher-ed-pew-finds.

27. Mangla, Ismat S. "Fearing 'indoctrination,' Parents in One US State Are Succeeding in Removing Islam from a School Curriculum." Quartz. Last modified September 29, 2016. https://qz.com/796141/tennessee-school-board-removes-section-on-islam-from-social studies-curriculum/.

28. Ismail, Aymann, and Jeffrey Bloomer. "Fox News Claimed a 'Sharia Court' Is Enforcing Islamic Law in Texas. So I Went to See It." Slate Magazine. Last modified October 13, 2017. https://slate.com/news-and-politics/2017/10/inside-a-sharia-law-court-in-texas.html.

29. Katersky, Aaron, and Chris Francescani. "4 Charged in Plot to Attack Upstate New York Muslim Community of Islamberg." ABC News. Last modified January 23, 2019. https://abcnews.go.com/US/charged-plot-attack-upstate-york-muslim-community-islamberg/story?id=60553265.

30. Graham, David A. "Why the Muslim 'No-Go-Zone' Myth Won't Die." The Atlantic. Last modified January 20, 2015. https://www.theatlantic.com/international/archive/2015/01/paris-mayor-to-sue-fox-over-no-go-zone-comments/384656/.

31. Ohlheiser, Abby. "Jeanine Pirro's anti-Muslim comments earned a rebuke from Fox News. They weren't her first." The Washington Post. Last modified March 11, 2019. https://www.washingtonpost.com/arts-entertainment/2019/03/11/jeanine-pirros-anti-muslim-comments-earned-rebuke-fox-news-they-werent-her-first/.

32. Frey, William H. "The US Will Become 'minority White' in 2045, Census Projects." Brookings. Last modified September 10, 2018. https://www.brookings.edu

/blog/the-avenue/2018/03/14/the-us-will-become-minority-white-in-2045-census-projects/.

33. Chinni, Dante. "Democrats' Popular Vote Edge is Growing. Will It Make a Difference?" NBC News. Last modified December 4, 2016. https://www.nbcnews.com/meet-the-press/popular-vote-advantage-democrats-continues-grow-n691266.

34. Surowiecki, James. 2004. *The Wisdom of Crowds: Why the Many are Smarter Than the Few and how Collective Wisdom Shapes Business, Economies, Societies, and Nations*. New York: Doubleday Books.

35. Clint, A. C. 2017. *The Art of Going Viral: 17 Studies to Reach Millions, Gain Influence, and Get Internet Famous*. Independently Published.

36. Ibid.

37. Zurcher, Anthony. "Trump's Anti-Muslim Retweet Fits a Pattern." BBC News. Last modified November 29, 2017. https://www.bbc.com/news/world-us-canada-42171550.

38. Marantz, Andrew. 2019. *Antisocial: Online Extremists, Techno-Utopians, and the Hijacking of the American Conversation*. New York: Viking, 18.

39. Ibid.

40. Ibid., 124.

41. Bail, Christopher A. 2016. *Terrified: How Anti-Muslim Fringe Organizations Became Mainstream*. Princeton: Princeton University Press.

42. Taleb, Nassim N. 2018. *Skin in the Game: Hidden Asymmetries in Daily Life*. New York: Random House.

Index

About the Author

Daniel Hummel received his doctorate in public administration from Florida Atlantic University in 2013. He is a faculty member at the University of Louisiana Monroe in the Department of Political Science. He teaches courses on state and local government, urban politics, research methods, intergovernmental relations, and other courses in the department. He researches issues of relevance to the Muslim American community. This includes the impacts of Islamophobia on this community.

www.ingramcontent.com/pod-product-compliance
Ingram Content Group UK Ltd.
Pitfield, Milton Keynes, MK11 3LW, UK
UKHW041844031026
15587UKWH00003B/990